Come *Walk* with Me

Come *Walk* with Me

A Woman's Personal Guide
to Knowing God
& Mentoring Others

Carole Mayhall

WATERBROOK
PRESS

COME WALK WITH ME
PUBLISHED BY WATERBROOK PRESS
12265 Oracle Boulevard, Suite 200
Colorado Springs, Colorado 80921

"Lord, You Know I'm Such a Stupid Sheep" from *Psalms of My Life*, Chariot Victor Publishing, copyright 1992. Used by permission of Chariot Victor Publishing.

Scriptures in this book, unless otherwise noted, are taken from the Holy Bible, New International Version copyright © 1973, 1978, 1984 International Bible Society. Used by permission of Zondervan Bible Publishers. Also quoted are the King James Version (KJV); New American Standard Bible (NASB) copyright © 1960, 1977 by the Lockman Foundation; The Living Bible (TLB) copyright © 1971 by Tyndale House Publishers; The New Testament in Modern English, Revised Edition (PH) copyright © 1972 by J. B. Phillips; The Holy Bible, New Living Translation (NLT) copyright © 1996 by Tyndale Charitable Trust; The Revised Standard Version Bible (RSV) copyright © 1946, 1973, Division of Christian Education, National Council of the Churches of Christ in the USA; The Amplified Bible (AMP), Old Testament, copyright © 1965, 1987 by the Zondervan Corporation. New Testament, copyright © 1954, 1958, 1987 by the Lockman Foundation. The New English Bible (NEB) copyright © 1961, 1970 by the Delegates of the Oxford University Press and the Syndics of the Cambridge University Press. All used by permission, all rights reserved.

ISBN 978-0-307-45887-2
ISBN 978-0-307-45940-4 (electronic)

Published in the United States by WaterBrook Multnomah, an imprint of the Crown Publishing Group, a division of Random House Inc., New York.

WATERBROOK and its deer colophon are registered trademarks of Random House Inc.

Library of Congress Cataloging-in-Publication Data
Mayhall, Carole.
    Come walk with me : a practical guide to knowing Christ intimately and passing it on / Carole Mayhall.—1st ed.
        p.   cm.
    Includes bibliographical references.
    1. Women—Religious life.   2. Discipling (Christianity)   3. Bible. N.T.
Titus II, 3-5—Criticism, interpretation, etc.   I. Title.
BV4527.M346   1998
248.8'43—dc21   97-42277
                                                                                                CIP

Printed in the United States of America
2012

10 9 8 7 6 5 4

SPECIAL SALES
Most WaterBrook Multnomah books are available at special quantity discounts when purchased in bulk by corporations, organizations, and special-interest groups. Custom imprinting or excerpting can also be done to fit special needs. For information, please e-mail SpecialMarkets@WaterBrookMultnomah.com or call 1-800-603-7051.

This book is dedicated to
Sonja,
dearest friend,
a woman with a heart for God
and a heart for His people.

CONTENTS

Where does one start when so many people have been involved in this project? But a few have helped more than they know.

Dan Rich of WaterBrook Press—who encouraged, believed in, and got behind this book. Thank you, Dan!

Liz Heaney—not just a good editor but a great one who helped shape, hone, and organize this book. She worked hard . . . and made me work hard, too, which made this book more readable.

My daughter, Lynn, my niece, Melody, and my friend, Sonja, who added examples from living with their children that helped me a great deal.

And for those who have allowed me to be a part of their lives—they helped me much more than I helped them!

And—I saved the best for last—my husband, Jack, who has spent hours brainstorming, listening, looking up references, and giving me massages when my back was aching from sitting at the computer all day. Thanks isn't adequate—I simply couldn't have done it without him!

CHAPTER ONE

Come Walk with Me

Excited! That word described Jack as he returned from a trip to Long Beach, California, to look over a new ministry opportunity. Like a kid telling about attending his first big league game, his eyes lit up as he described what he had discovered about the job. We'd be moving into a large old home already furnished and occupied by four men, one woman, a couple in an apartment out back, and oh, yes, a dachshund. The people currently in charge couldn't take the dog with them to Okinawa, so they were leaving him with us. And (he threw it in quickly, hoping I wouldn't notice) the dog wasn't quite housebroken.

Jack and I would be responsible for helping men and women grow in spiritual maturity, ministry skills, and life skills; ministering to servicemen coming through a servicemen's center; raising a budget that was several thousand dollars in the hole; opening our home for hospitality . . . As Jack rambled on and on, my eyes glazed over and my mind went numb. He had no idea the effect all this was having on me, of course. But the longer he talked, the more the task looked as impossible as crawling around the world without legs!

When Jack finished telling me about this glorious opportunity we were going to have in Long Beach, I went upstairs to our bedroom, got down on my knees, and prayed, "Father! You've just heard it all. And You know *I can't do it!*

"You also know that of all the things I *don't* want to do, the number one item is to fail Jack in something You have called him to do—and it seems You are calling him to do this. But obviously I'm going to fail both him and You in this.

"So . . . ," I paused before committing myself to what I was about to ask. "I think You'd better take me home to Yourself *right now*. Then Jack can marry someone who *will* be able to help him with this task."

With tremor of heart, I waited. In expectation, I waited . . . fully anticipating that God would strike me dead on the spot. But no bolt of lightning came from the sky. No heart attack or blood clot to the brain. After ten minutes or so, I concluded that God was going to leave me among the living.

Perplexed, I prayed, "All right then, Father, if You aren't going to take me home, then You'll have to help me grow into . . . to become somehow . . . the person You need in this situation."

And God began to answer that prayer through a godly woman who taught me, trained me, and in a real way, "titused" me (see Titus 2:3-5).

Shortly after we moved to that big old white house on Willow Avenue in Long Beach, I began driving the frenzied freeways up to Pasadena each week. Every Wednesday morning I'd put our three-year-old daughter, Lynn, in the car, and off we'd go. I'd only learned to drive about six months before, and the heavy traffic scared me to death. But I was desperate for help—and determined—so I would grit my teeth and head into the fray.

An hour or so later I'd pull into the driveway of an even bigger old house in Pasadena where Marion lived. Marion, the wife of Jack's supervisor, was only about five years older than I was but light years more mature spiritually—and she had agreed to disciple me. She and I would closet ourselves in her spacious bedroom for a couple of hours, made possible with help from a girl working in Marion's home who watched Lynn and Marion's son, Ricky.

I said to Marion, "Pretend I'm not even a Christian. Lead me to Christ, and then teach me everything I need to know in order to grow. And please teach me in such a way that I will be able to pass on to others what I learn."

And for one year Marion did just that. She taught me everything from how to share the gospel and dig into Scripture and pray, to how to cook for twenty people. I needed to learn *everything!* Marion walked beside me and imprinted my life with marks of the Savior.

As I have grown spiritually, God has given me the privilege of walking beside a number of women from different backgrounds and situations: women raised in Christian homes and ones who have come to know Christ as adults; women from uncomplicated backgrounds and ones from dysfunctional families; happily married women and others in hurting relationships. Many floundered because they hadn't been helped to find practical, shoe-leather ways to live *joyfully*.

I remember the young single teacher who had been violated as a child by a relative, leaving her unable to know both God's joy and a husband's love.

Then there was Norma, who tried to take her own life by overdosing on sleeping pills. God had never become real in her life.

I think of the young widow with six children who tearfully told me that God had given her the gift of introducing people to Christ—even over the phone—but she didn't know how to help them move forward in their Christian walk.

I reflect on the wives and single women who longed to know God intimately but didn't know *how*.

In their individual ways, each of these women said to me, "God promises joy, but I don't have it. What's wrong?"

Let me tell you about one woman in particular.

ARE YOU FOR REAL?

Sonja stood on my doorstep five inches below me, her laughing blue eyes level with mine. A breeze ruffled her blonde wedge and, noting the lithe body in blue-and-wine sweats, I guessed she was on the shy side of thirty. Curious to find out the reason she'd asked to see me, I invited her in.

After settling on the couch, she took a deep breath and plunged in. Her first question came out of the blue, and I blinked.

"Are you for real?" she asked.

"What do you mean?"

"Well, I heard you speak a couple of weeks ago, and I couldn't quite believe what I heard."

I raised questioning eyebrows, and she continued. "I'm the wife of a full-time Christian worker. I teach the Bible, and the people in my group think I've got it all together. But . . . ," She pulled at a strand of hair, paused, and looked away. Then, making a conscious and determined decision to be open with me—a stranger—she continued. "They don't know *me*—not the real inside me. It's all a facade."

She produced a superficial grin as though to cover up the intensity of her feelings and blurted, "You said the kind of peace and joy I'm looking for are found by dwelling deeply in the Word of God. I've never experienced real peace and joy. I had to come to ask you if what you said is really true."

And so began a relationship with Sonja, which started with my teaching her some foundational truths about an active relationship with God, progressed to training her in aspects of life and godliness, and grew into the deepest of friendships. We've prayed together, cried together, ministered together, played together. Mentoring, mothering, counseling, discipling—we've been through it all. In the process, I gained more than I gave, learned more than I taught, and today I praise God for the joy she's been—and is—to me.

Our relationship has been the fullest kind of Titus 2 relationship. And that's the kind of relationship that I long for each of you to enjoy.

DON'T MISS OUT!

When Paul wrote to Titus, he said all Christians need to learn certain basic truths. Then he singled out four groups who were to *major* on a few other essential qualities. For example, the old men were to be worthy of respect (among other things); the younger men needed to learn self-control; the slaves were to be submissive; and the older women were to learn reverence. But Paul added another group when he spoke to the "older women." He said that they were to teach the *younger women* about seven critical issues spelled out in Titus 2:3-5. These are so important, I've covered each one in a separate chapter in Part Two.

Before learning about these character issues, however, we need to know and understand the essentials that are important for *all* Christians. Without a firm foundation in these basics of the Christian life (covered in Part One), we'll go nowhere toward becoming the godly women we long to be. If we are not convinced of the absolute importance of Christ being the center of our lives, of His Word being essential to our growth, of obeying what He says, and of seeking God in prayer, then we'll never have the strength, power, or desire to be godly women.

I've had a number of unhealthy fears throughout my life, but there's one fear I hope I'll never lose: the fear of missing out on something God wants for me to know and experience *right here on earth*. I'm guessing that you don't want to miss out on anything either—that you long to be *excited* about God and your Christian life and to experience the joys of God's Word.

But how? That's the question, isn't it? The *what, when*, and *who* are important, but the *how* is crucial. I hope that this book will give you some hands-on help for how to become the kind of woman you want to be—and who the Lord of the universe longs for you to be.

HEART TO HEART . . .

Many women have no one to teach them—to walk beside them and help them experience the joy that comes from knowing God intimately. I wish I could sit down with each one of you personally and talk face to face about the essentials of your relationship with God. But sharing my heart through the pages of this book is my next best choice. These chapters contain what I've sought to teach women over the years concerning God's truth and godly living.

Because discipleship is meant to be a relationship, it's always best if you can sit down with a person and talk over your questions as well as be held accountable for your actions. For that reason, I encourage you to look for a mature Christian woman—young or old—who might be willing to go through this book with you. But don't be discouraged if you can't find someone. Don't let that stop you from pursuing God on your own.

At the end of the chapters I've included a section called "Making Biblical Truth Yours," which includes studies and assignments you can do to help yourself grow and develop in areas critical for spiritual maturity. There are more studies than you may want to do, but I've included them for a reason. Weaker areas of our lives need more attention than stronger areas. For example, if you were born a gentle person, you may need to spend only a week or two on the subject of gentleness. But if you've struggled with a lack of gentleness all your life, you'll need to spend weeks or even months developing it. (Would you believe the rest of your life?)

When I asked Sonja to do a simple study and call me when she finished, I heard her laughing voice on the phone within a week: "I've finished the assignment. What's next?"

"Ah," I said to myself. "Maybe . . . just maybe . . . she's a learner." And she was. And since you're reading this book, you must be, too! I suggest that first you read it straight through for an overview of the content. Then go back to chapter two and begin again, taking as much time as you need to do the studies at the end of each chapter.

It will be a great privilege for me if you will walk beside me to explore what it takes to become first a godly woman, then a "Titus" woman, and finally a woman who has the heart and ability to reach out and help, or "titus," another. So please . . . come walk with me. Walk beside me. And let's explore . . . together.

CHAPTER TWO

Who's on First?

The Importance of Christ

I sat across the table from a friend of mine, and for three hours I listened to her problems . . . and my friend has problems. Probably for the fifteenth time, I listened to my friend's problems. So, when she took a deep breath, I broke in.

"Friend, let me ask you something. If you were to draw a circle that represents your life, what would be in the center?"

After a long moment she murmured, "My problems."

And she spoke the truth.

A week later I sat by the hospital bed of my younger sister, Joye, who had just been diagnosed with acute lymphatic leukemia. Her face was death-gray and moist with perspiration, and a swath of bandages encased her throat. A student nurse came to interview Joye about her "stress experience." This young woman was interviewing terminally ill patients to see if, in some way, she might be able to help them.

I heard my sister, her face lit from within, say, "Oh, Jan. I'm not afraid of death. I'm a bit fearful of the pain and process of dying, but I'm not afraid of *death*. It will just be a change of residence for me."

And for forty-five minutes Joye explained the good news of Jesus Christ to Jan.

Later I thought, *Both my sister and my friend have problems. Yet one is full of despair, the other full of joy. What makes the difference?* And then it dawned on me. My friend's heart was occupied with her problems; my sister's heart was occupied with the living God. And that made all the difference in the world.

WE NEED THE RIGHT CENTER

What does it mean to have our hearts occupied with God? Many of us give lip service to that truth and say that God is the center of our lives, but our actions and thoughts reveal something radically different. We need a center. Our lives require a hub, a weight-bearing center around which everything else revolves. Often, however, we live with weak and flimsy hubs—or no hubs at all.

As I was contemplating this recently, I had an imaginary conversation with three women: a graduate student, an attractive professional, and a young stay-at-home mom. (The nice thing about imaginary conversations is that everyone says exactly what you want them to!) The interview went something like this:

Me (to student): May I ask you something personal? What has been your primary focus in the past year? Around what do your thoughts revolve?

Student: Why, my studies, my education. That has to be my primary focus for now.

Me (to mom): What about you? What is at the center of your time and thoughts?

Mom (with a tired sigh): My family. My children and my husband . . . and my home, too, I guess. They take the vast majority of my time and thoughts these days.

Me (to professional who looked every bit as sophisticated as she was): And you?

Professional (thoughtfully): Well, I'm absorbed in my career—and I love it! But God is important in my life, too.

Mom and *Student* (in unison): Oh, I didn't mean to say that He isn't important to me as well.

Professional: I guess if I'm going to be absolutely honest, I'd say that my time revolves around my career, but my heart is divided between that career and God.

Me (to student): What happens when you graduate? What will be your focus then?

Student: I really don't know.

Me (to mom): And when your children are grown? Or if they disappoint you? If your husband is unfaithful or dies? What then?

Mom (shuddering): Oh, I can't think about that!

Me (to professional): Tell me, how does a wheel that has two hubs operate?

Professional (laughing a bit nervously): Unevenly! Not very balanced, for sure.

My imaginary conversation faded, and my thoughts grew serious. In order to operate effectively, a wheel needs a center, or hub, and like that wheel, my life needs a sturdy center to provide stability. If my life centers around my family or friends, they inevitably will disappoint me or leave. If my life revolves around a sport, hobby, or career, it won't hold up in the latter years of my life. Nothing is worthy to be the center of my life except that which is strong, lasting, and balanced.

There is only one who meets those qualifications: Christ Himself. He can bear the weight of my life, take the strain, and maintain the balance. Without this sure foundation, my life may crack, shatter, splinter, or fall apart; but with the solidity of this Rock, my life will be stable and secure. Psalm 18:2 declares, "The LORD is my rock, my fortress and my deliverer; my God is my rock, in whom I take refuge."

I recently met a woman whose life exemplified this.

First, I observed her radiant smile.

Second, I noticed she was in a wheelchair.

Third, I saw she had no legs.

As we talked after the meeting, I discovered that severe diabetes hindered her circulation. She'd wounded herself while cutting her toenails, and an infection developed, causing gangrene to set in. Ultimately, her legs had to be amputated above the knees.

I murmured, "I can't even imagine the pain and suffering you've experienced."

Her smile grew even more radiant, and she hesitated not a moment. "Oh," she protested, "but I still have *Jesus!*"

Why did her response amaze me? Perhaps because she was wrapped up in the middle of a truth of which most of us clutch only a small piece.

WHAT IS YOUR CENTER?

Self-examination time. (Don't worry, friend—no one is going to grade you.)

First of all, think back over the past month of your life. What did you think about most?

Second, when life's ripples become waves, to whom do you turn? To whom do you pour out your heart and thoughts?

Third, when you think about the verse "If anyone would come after me, he must deny himself and take up his cross daily and follow me. For whoever wants to save his life will lose it, but whoever loses his life for me will save it" (Luke 9:23-24), do you feel more than a little uncomfortable? I think all of us squirm a bit on that one, but our hearts may condemn us to the extreme if we aren't willing to make Christ the Lord and center of our lives.

I've heard it said that the Christian life is one great big YES and a lot of little uh-huhs. The big yes is when we receive Christ as our Savior, and the little uh-huhs come as we obey and grow.

I think that's the way it is when it comes to knowing God. First we have to admit our need to know Him, and then we have to take the steps to do that. It takes a lifetime, of course, and because His character is limitless, we'll be learning for all eternity.

WHO IS GOD?

Who is God to you? Please take a moment right now and write down some characteristics of God you have *personally* observed. (Wish we could go over your list together!)

Psalm 62:11-12 says, "One thing God has spoken, two things have I heard: that you, O God, are strong, and that you, O Lord, are loving." It's curious that God spoke one thing and the psalmist heard two. Obviously God looks at the two characteristics mentioned here as so intertwined as to be one, but the psalmist separates them: God is *strong*, and God is *loving*. Because He is strong, He is *able* to be involved in every detail of my life. Because He is loving, He is *willing* to be involved in every detail of my life. That's incredible!

In order to have our hearts occupied with God and to know Him in a deep way, we must catch a glimpse of how *big* He really is—to look until we're quickened with joy at the wonder and awesomeness of the Lord. Often I look into a clear night sky and am reminded of the vastness of God's creation. I love Genesis 1:16 where it says that God created the sun and the moon, and then, almost in an aside adds, "He also made the stars." (Can you imagine that the creation of billions of stars is summed up in five words?)

But as awed as I am at the vastness of the universe, I think I'm just as amazed at the microscopic world inside me. In their book *Fearfully and Wonderfully Made*, Dr. Paul Brand and Philip Yancey say that each of us is comprised of a hundred trillion cells, each flooded with information about the rest of the body. The uniqueness of each individual lies locked away inside each cell nucleus, chemically coiled in a strand of DNA. Once an egg and sperm share their inheritance, the DNA chemical ladder splits down the center of every gene much as the teeth of a zipper pull apart. DNA re-forms itself each time the cell divides—each new cell containing identical DNA. Along the way cells specialize, but each carries the entire instruction book of one hundred thousand genes. DNA is estimated to contain instructions that, if written out, would fill a thousand six-hundred-page books! Each cell possesses a genetic code so complete that the entire body could be reassembled from information in any one of the body's cells. The DNA is so narrow and compacted that all the genes in all the body's cells would fit into an ice cube, yet if the DNA were unwound and joined together end to end, the strand could stretch from the earth to the sun and back more than four hundred times![1]

That is the bigness of God.

He is big, strong . . . but also loving. The disciple John felt free to lay his head on Jesus' breast, and in doing so, he could *hear* His whisper. He could listen to His heartbeat. I need to learn to do that, too. I need to *know* about His love in order to *feel* that love.

KNOWING GOD'S LOVE

Periodically over the years, I've asked God to teach me one new thing about Himself each week—or deepen a truth I already know. That's been a wonderful experience. I'll never forget one week in which I kept hearing God's voice saying one word to my soul. The word was *beloved.* All week He whispered that word to my heart, and it deepened my certainty of His love for me. When I was feeling useless, He would say, "Beloved." When I was feeling harried, I'd hear Him whisper, "Beloved." When I was anxious and cross, He would say it, too. All week long, my heart heard Him until I *felt* loved. He deepened my understanding of a truth I already knew.

Meditating on verses about God's love is also a good way to make this truth real. Read Ephesians 1:3-14 every day for one week. Write out verses 7 and 8 and leave them as a bookmark in your Bible to read each day for several weeks. These verses say, "In him we have redemption through his blood, the forgiveness of sins, in accordance with the riches of God's grace that he lavished on us with all wisdom and understanding." Don't you love that? God lavishes His grace and love on us in more ways than a doting mother or a newly-in-love fiancé or a generous benefactor does.

I need to know that God is great, and I need to know that part of that greatness is His willingness and ability to love me personally. And in Christ, He does.

Let's take another step down the path. Colossians 1:12-22 enumerates seven significant aspects of what God has done for me as His child. As I thought about them, this allegory came to me.

Her mother deserted her before she was a week old, and she grew up in a tenement with an abusive, evil father. She had her father's temper and learned from childhood his ways of violence, anger, cruelty, selfishness, jealousy, intolerance, and deceitfulness. Deep inside her soul, she knew she was headed for self-destruction.

Occasionally, she would wander across town and peer in through the high fence of a huge wealthy estate and catch glimpses of the fantastic mansion within. Sometimes she'd dream of living there, but of course, it could never be possible for someone like her.

However, one day she met a person who, for some inconceivable reason, wanted to be her friend. Kind in the face of her cruelty, compassionate to her constant combativeness, tender as she treated him terribly, he demonstrated consistent love and continued to be her friend.

One incredible day he told her that he was the son of the wealthy man who owned the vast estate across town, and he made her an offer that she found quite unbelievable. He said, "I'd like you to become a part of my family—to be my sister and share in my inheritance. If you are willing, I'll give you a new family, a fresh start, and a brand-new life."

"But why would you do that?" she asked, trembling.

"Because I love you," he replied.

"But how can you do that?" she questioned.

"This may sound strange, but my father has qualified you to come into my family," he said. "And I've already paid the price to buy your freedom from your abusive father—I've redeemed you, and I've forgiven you for all the things you've done. All you have to do is accept my offer."

She couldn't believe what she was hearing! But she knew she had nothing to lose and everything to gain. So she held out her hand to take his, and suddenly—in one astonishing moment—she was a member of his family, the daughter of the richest man in the world, forgiven and loved. She—at long last—belonged!

She belonged, but she had so much to learn . . . about her new father, about his son, about her new family. She was loved, but she had to learn how to be loving. She was valued, but she had to learn to value others. She had entered into a new world, obtained a new position, and been adopted into a new family. It would take the rest of her life to learn to become the kind of person who could reflect and honor the one who had made all this possible. She determined to begin!

All the truths in this allegory come out of Colossians, which explains that God has—

- qualified me to share in his inheritance (1:12)
- rescued me from the dominion of darkness (1:13)
- brought me into the kingdom of the Son He loves (1:13)
- redeemed me (1:14)
- forgiven me of my sins (1:14)
- reconciled me (1:20-21)
- freed me from any accusation (1:22)

Have you given serious thought to these magnificent truths? If not, you may want to make a deeper study of each one by looking up key words such as *inheritance, redemption,* and *reconciliation* in a concordance. And if the wonder of your salvation has faded, if you have a ho-hum attitude about being a child of God, pray Psalm 51:12: "Restore to me the joy of your salvation."

In order to have hearts occupied with God, to have Christ as the hub and center of our lives, to experience His wonder and joy, we must continue to plumb the depths of who He is and of His love for us.

FALLING IN LOVE WITH CHRIST

How do we fall more deeply in love with Christ? The same way we fall in love with a person.

After Jack and I met at college, we wanted to get to know each other better, so we spent every free hour we had with each other. We met between classes, we studied together (well, sort of studied together), ate our meals together, went places together. We talked. We observed the other in every situation, met each other's families, got acquainted with each other's friends. We talked. I asked questions and learned about football because Jack was a quarterback on the football team. He listened to me practice on the piano. And we talked.

As I observed how he acted toward me, his family, and others, how he responded in various situations, what he thought about both deep and superficial things, my respect for him grew. Our friendship deepened. And our love blossomed.

Did we argue? Yes. Did we fight? Yes. Over the years, we've been through some tough times, both in our relationship and in our lives. But we never shut the other out. And each year our love has deepened. Friendship and love developed from spending time together, talking, and doing pleasurable things together.

Love for the Lord develops in much the same way: spending time together (we'll talk about that in the next two chapters), talking with Him (in prayer, discussed in chapter five), and experiencing life together.

The girl in my allegory realized that becoming an authentic member of a wealthy family was a lifelong process. Like her, we need to understand that becoming royalty inside and out—being the daughter of the King—will take the rest of our lives. To become like the King, or "God-like" (godly), is a process accomplished only by living in His house, "eating" His food (the Word of God), studying His character, asking forgiveness when we fail, and begging for help to progress. It means staying focused on Christ and making Him the very center of our thoughts and lives. Difficult? Surely. Impossible, actually, without His Spirit dwelling in us, leading us, counseling us, helping us. "With man this is impossible, but with God all things are possible" (Matthew 19:26).

The bottom line is found in Ephesians 3:14-19, which *The Living Bible* translates:

When I think of the wisdom and scope of his plan I fall down on my knees and pray . . . that out of his glorious, unlimited resources he will give you the mighty inner strengthening of his Holy Spirit. And I pray that Christ will be more and more at home in your hearts, living within you as you trust in him. May your roots go down deep into the soil of God's marvelous love; and may you be able to feel and understand, as all God's children should, how long, how wide, how deep, and how high his love really is; and to experience this love for yourselves, though it is so great that you will never see the end of it or fully know or understand it. And so at last you will be filled up with God himself.

According to these verses we are "filled up with God" when we are wide open to the Holy Spirit (not allowing any "dark corners" to remain in our hearts) and know the love of Christ. *The Living Bible* gives three words for the word translated *know* in other versions: *feel, understand,* and *experience.* We feel with our hearts, we understand with our minds, and we experience with our lives. When we feel Christ, when we understand His love, when we experience the marvelous things He has for us, our hearts will become more and more focused on things above, and Christ will be the hub of our lives.

I can personally testify to the fact that knowing the theology of the Bible won't make Christ central in our lives. There's much more to it than that. God commands, "in your hearts set apart Christ as Lord" (1 Peter 3:15). I wish I could give you some shortcuts. But I can't.

The story is told of a violinist who gave an extraordinary performance one evening. A man came up to him afterward and said, "Oh,

I'd give my life to be able to play like that." The violinist looked him straight in the eye and said, "I have."

Yes, it will take all our lives. But friend, let me ask you: What else is worth giving your life for?

If we make it our goal to focus on the Lord Christ, then when the typhoon of adversity hits us, slamming us into rocks of pain and despair, perhaps we will be able to smile radiantly and declare—as did the woman who had no legs—"Oh, but you see, I still have *Jesus!*"

And He is enough.

Making Biblical Truth Yours

You've now come to what will be the most important part of this book. God doesn't promise that what I say will make a difference in your life. He promises that His Word won't return empty but will accomplish what He pleases (Isaiah 55:11). His Word is a sharp sword (Hebrews 4:12), a hammer (Jeremiah 23:29), a fire (Jeremiah 20:9), a light (Psalm 119:105), and most important, the way to insight (Psalm 119:99), understanding (Psalm 119:130), and spiritual growth (1 Peter 2:2-3; 2 Peter 1:3-8). So please, my friend, don't hurry through these studies. Do each assignment prayerfully and carefully. You will get out of them exactly what you put in.

My goal is to give you several methods of study that can be done on your own or with a group. These won't be difficult to learn but undoubtedly will be demanding on your life. The most precious and life-changing part of these studies is the personal application—and let me assure you, the Enemy of your soul will try his best to defeat you on this. He doesn't want your life to change, but God does. It will take much prayer and discipline to do that part of the study regularly.

You'll need a good translation of the Bible. A translation is different from a paraphrase. Bible translations are done by a group of scholars working to translate the original Hebrew (Old Testament) and Greek (New Testament) texts into another language. A paraphrase, on the other hand, is usually the work of one person putting either the original or a *translation* into his own words. For devotional reading, paraphrased Bibles such as the *Phillips* version, *The Living Bible,* or *The Message* can give wonderful insights, but to get the more exact meaning of the text, stick to a true translation like the *New King James Version,* the *New American Standard Bible,* or the *New International Version.*

The first type of study I suggest you learn is a simple verse analysis. Then I'll show you how to do a personal application study.

How to Do a Verse Study

You can study a couple of verses or a whole paragraph. Before you begin a verse study, read the entire chapter of the Bible in which it is located, or at least the paragraph before and after the verse. This will help prevent you from taking a verse out of its context, or setting, and misinterpreting its message. When you feel you have an understanding of the context, then you can study the individual verse.

Here are the basic elements of a verse study:

What does it say?
Write out the verse in your own words. This is called *paraphrasing.*

What does the verse say that I don't understand?
Write down the questions you have about the meaning of the verse.

What does it say somewhere else?
Using a concordance, look up other scriptures that might shed light on the verse. Both *Cruden's* and *Strong's* are good concordances, but most translations of the Bible have developed one specifically for that translation. Many Bibles also have a very brief concordance in the back, and some give other pertinent references in a middle margin. A study Bible such as the *Ryrie Study Bible* (Moody Press), the *Oxford NIV Scofield Study Bible* (Oxford University Press), the *NIV Study Bible* (Zondervan), or the *Thompson Chain-Reference Study Bible* (Kirkbride) might be a good investment as well.

What does it say to me?
Ask God to show you something from the verse that you can apply to your life this week.

A Sample Verse Study

Let's do a verse study together on Matthew 6:33: "But seek first his kingdom and his righteousness, and all these things will be given to you as well."

What does it say?
My paraphrase: If I put God and His goodness first in my life, He will take care of everything else.

What does it say that I don't understand?
What does "his righteousness" mean?

What does "God's kingdom" mean?

Does this verse mean that He'll provide everything I need without having to work?

Does it mean my wants as well as needs?

What does it say somewhere else?

Luke 9:23-25 says that if anyone would follow Christ, he must deny himself and take up his cross daily. It also asks what good it is if a man gains the whole world and yet loses his very self.

Matthew 10:38 says that anyone who doesn't take his cross and follow Christ isn't worthy of Him.

What does it say to me?

This verse says to me that everything else in the world pales in comparison to Christ and the importance of following Him with all my heart. But I don't always do that in my life, especially in the area of time; I waste a lot of time on inconsequential things. This week I'm going to jot down the hours I spend doing various things and ask God for insight into how I spend my time. At the end of the week I'll go over my schedule and see what needs to be changed.

Working with this basic outline, let's do a few more verse studies, perhaps two or three each week. Here are some suggestions:

On who Christ is:

- Hebrews 1:3-4
- John 1:1 (Read John 1:1-14 before you begin this one.)
- John 14:6

On the importance of following Him:

- Luke 18:29-30
- Matthew 16:24-26

How to Do a Personal Application Study

Remember, the most important part of any study is applying it. One of the tools that helped my Christian life get off a plateau and start going straight up was the personal application outline I started to do with every Bible study.

When God whispers to your heart, "This is for you," take these steps:

Write the verse or verses out in your own words. (You've already done that with a verse study.)

Write how you've failed to obey this verse. (Use *I, me, my,* not *we* or *us.*)

Give a specific illustration. (Pull one from your *recent* past.)

After asking God for His wisdom, *make a "plan of attack" to begin to obey this verse.* Whatever you do, it should be something that can be done this week. If at all possible, have someone check your progress next week.

You should do only one application study per week, or you'll soon be working on so many you'll get discouraged and quit. In each application, concentrate on doing specific things that can be accomplished in one week. God may continue to lay that subject on your heart next week, but He will give you additional steps to focus on that week—one step at a time.

One thing you should always consider doing is memorizing the verse you're studying, asking God to bring it to mind regularly during the week. Another is putting it on the top of your prayer list for one week. Other suggestions will be given throughout this book.

I'm excited about what God is going to teach you in the weeks and months ahead!

CHAPTER THREE

Essentially Yours

The Importance of God's Word

Obviously, Lois had been crying. Even now her red-rimmed eyes blinked rapidly to keep the tears from flowing as she explained, "A coworker just told me she thinks I act aloof and superior. I feel like punching her out!"

"What's stopping you?" I questioned.

She smiled grimly. "Because I know the Lord won't let me get away with it!"

Lois and I had been studying the Bible together for some time, and I watched to see what would happen. A couple of weeks later, I found out.

"What happened with your coworker?" I asked.

"Well, of course, I had to pray!" Lois confessed. "And then I had to see what God wanted my response to be, right?"

I nodded.

"During the past two weeks as I went to the Bible, I read things like, 'But how is it to your credit if you receive a beating for doing wrong and endure it? But if you suffer for doing good and you endure it, this is commendable before God. To this you were called, because Christ suffered for you, leaving you an example, that you should follow in his steps. . . . When they hurled their insults at him, he did not retaliate' (1 Peter 2:20-21, 23). And, 'Be completely humble and gentle; be patient, bearing with one another in love. Make every effort to keep the unity of the Spirit through the bond of peace' (Ephesians 4:2-3). I realized God was asking me not to retaliate but to be kind."

"So what's the next step?" I asked.

"I've already taken it. After I'd prayed, I went back to her and apologized for anything I'd done that gave her the impression I felt superior. I told her I *didn't* feel superior and I wasn't aware of what I was doing to appear aloof. Then I asked her to give me specific examples of what I did that gave that impression. She couldn't think of any right then, so I asked her to tell me the next time I did or said something to cause her to feel I was being superior."

"Wow!" I said. "You're really opening yourself up for some possibly painful times, aren't you?"

"Yes," she said slowly. "I thought about that. But recently God has shown me that I need to be more vulnerable and open to changing areas of my life that are weak or wrong. I think this could be part of His answer."

My admiration for Lois grew a ton! We had been studying how important God's Word is—not only for doctrine but for life—and she was really putting it into practice.

Some months later, I had to be reminded of the same lesson.

WHAT DO I HAVE TO OFFER OTHERS?

The petite brunette came into my hotel room and collapsed in the overstuffed chair. As she poured out her heart to me, sobs punctuated her story. I struggled not to look shocked, but her tale of years of abuse as a child was so appalling that I sat numb. And dumb. The next day the Father and I had a long, tearful talk about that conversation.

"Father, help me, please!" I prayed. "I talk to more and more women these days with broken lives, women who are emotionally destitute, who feel unloved and seem shattered beyond repair. You have allowed me the privilege of being a teacher to some. But how can I teach them? I've never been where they've been, experienced what they've experienced. How can I possibly help? I feel inadequate to lead another study or speak to another group of women or write another page. What should I do?"

God never stops surprising me! This was one of those times He answered almost before I got the words out of my mouth. My Bible reading that morning was Psalm 19, and verses 7-11 spoke as though the mighty voice of God heralded me from the burning bush:

> The law of the LORD is perfect, reviving the soul.
> The statutes of the LORD are trustworthy, making wise
> the simple.
> The precepts of the LORD are right, giving joy to the heart.
> The commands of the LORD are radiant, giving light to
> the eyes.
> The fear of the LORD is pure, enduring forever.
> The ordinances of the LORD are sure and altogether
> righteous.
> They are more precious than gold, than much pure gold;
> They are sweeter than honey, than honey from the comb.
> By them is your servant warned; in keeping them there is
> great reward.

The Father said to my heart, "You forget, beloved, that the greatest wisdom of people is foolishness to Me. Even if you had so many degrees in education that the credentials ran right off the page, your wisdom still wouldn't hold a candle to Mine. True, you aren't a doctor in counseling, you've never received a Ph.D. in studies concerning human nature, and you are, well, simple. But take heart and listen to what I'm telling you. My Word makes wise the simple. Your friends are like women everywhere; they need joy, light, purpose, wisdom, direction, peace. And this is exactly what My Word gives. You don't need to have 'the answers' because My Word is the answer. So, child, keep it simple. Just give them My Word."

Whew! As I got up from my knees, my heart was light. Though I knew I would struggle periodically with teaching, speaking, and writing, God assured me that having the wisdom to help people lies in tapping into *His* wisdom—which He says I can do when I know His Word. It is *His Word* that will give joy . . . peace to troubled hearts . . . answers for desperate needs.

Most of us have no idea of the magnitude, the significance, the importance of God's Word. We may believe that it's beneficial, but we haven't grasped that it's *essential*, absolutely *critical* for our lives and for our growth. We may believe with our minds, but the truth hasn't become a part of our lives.

So let's go back to that psalm and think it through together.

GOD'S WORD IS FULL OF BENEFITS

Psalm 19 lists several things God's Word *is* and *does* that should make anyone want to hold on to it as tightly as to life itself. God's Word is

- perfect (v. 7)
- trustworthy (v. 7)
- right (v. 8)
- radiant (v. 8)
- sure and righteous (altogether right and true) (v. 9)
- precious (priceless) (v. 10)
- sweet (v. 10)

And listen to some of the things it does:

- revives the soul (v. 7)
- makes the simple wise (v. 7)
- gives joy to the heart (v. 8)
- gives light to the eyes (v. 8)

Let's look at these four benefits one at a time.

"The law of the LORD is perfect, reviving the soul."
I doubt there is a woman among us who hasn't been depressed or discouraged. Well, I have good news for you. God's Word *revives* (makes alive, lifts up, brightens) the soul. I know. Let me tell you about a time it revived me.

Way down in my heart I knew—without a shadow of a doubt—that I couldn't handle what lay ahead. The countries sounded exotic; I was excited about visiting them, anticipating the ministry opportunities outlined. But I was scared to death. Jack and I would be away from home for two months in places with names like Kotakinabalu and Kuching. Strange customs. Strange food. Strange lands. Among godly people who had suffered for their faith. What gave me reason to think that I might be able to minister to them? Obviously, Jack and I would learn from them, but we were supposed to be the teachers.

Two days before we were to fly to Asia, I dashed to the store for some milk. As I turned the key in the ignition, I heard Sandi Patty's voice on the car radio. That glorious voice sang straight to my heart, and the words were God's Word. Over and over she sang, "Go in the strength of the Lord," and if I'd been shot with pure adrenaline, it couldn't have done to me what those words did. I was reminded that I didn't have to go on that trip depending solely on my small store of wisdom. I could go in the strength of Him who has all power and authority and majesty.

Right then and there—in my small red Honda—God's Word revived my soul. It wasn't the first time. Nor will it be the last. But nothing else could have revived my soul in the same way. Nothing.

When you are feeling down, discouraged, or depressed, ask God for special sensitivity to hear Him with the ears of your heart. Then you'll be more alert to the many means He has at His disposal to revive your soul, whether it's a word from a friend, a song, or a special touch as you read His Word.

I remember flying home after spending an extremely difficult time with an emotionally ill friend. I felt exhausted, wiped out mentally and physically, and dull. The pilot had to skirt some storm clouds, and as we circled close to them, I gasped. The colors in those clouds were like nothing I'd ever seen from the earth or the sky. Brilliant red, purple, pink, orange, and violet clouds were momentarily split apart by jagged flashes of lightning. For twenty minutes I watched in awe and wonder as God brought the verse to mind: "The heavens declare the glory of God" (Psalm 19:1). I arrived home refreshed, revived, and revitalized. The beauty of creation and the words of Psalm 19 reminded me that the God of the universe is in charge of the world—as well as my friend's situation.

"The statutes of the LORD are trustworthy, making wise the simple."
This verse encourages me because I feel so in need of wisdom. Left to my own resources, I sometimes feel like I wouldn't know what to do or say in certain situations. I was reminded of my need for wisdom when, with concern in her voice, Wanda asked the $100,000 question: "Carole, why is it that women don't seem to respond to me?"

How in the world would I know? I thought. And yet . . . I had a hard time talking to her, too. Why? Wanda longed to help disciple younger women. Yet the women she wanted to pour her life into seemed reluctant. They asked her to help them and then, like silent shadows, drifted away. What was she doing wrong? I mumbled some inadequate answer and changed the subject.

But I did begin to pray about her dilemma. And that very week as I was reading Proverbs, one verse gave me the answer. It said, "As in water face answereth to face, so the heart of man to man" (Proverbs 27:19, KJV). "Face answereth to face. . . ." The words revolved slowly in my mind. *What does that mean?* Suddenly I knew what Wanda's problem was—and God's Word had provided the answer.

You've heard of a monotone voice? Well, Wanda had a monotone face. Hers rarely registered emotion. I always felt uncomfortable talking with her because I constantly wondered how she was reacting to what I was saying. When she was talking, it wasn't much better. I couldn't help wondering if she even cared about what she was telling me for there was no animation, no excitement, no *spark*.

I prayed about whether I should talk to her about her lack of facial expression, and God gave me the green light. So the next time we were together I said, "You know, Wanda, there's a verse in the Bible that says, 'face answers to face.' In other words, we reflect back what we see as we talk to another person. But your face doesn't do that. I think it could be the reason women aren't responding to you. You have the wisdom, the godliness, the desire to help others, but they can't read that in your face. Do you want me to pray with you for God's help as you begin working on your facial expression?" She said she did. In the following months, her face became more animated, and talking with her became easier. I noticed her ministry to women grew as well. God, through His Word, gave me wisdom I didn't have.

How exactly does He do this? He answers our requests for wisdom by giving us insight into His Word through His Holy Spirit. In this particular instance, I started with His promises and memorized two verses: Psalm 19:7, which I've already mentioned, and James 1:5, which says, "If any of you lacks wisdom, he should ask God, who gives generously to all without finding fault, and it will be given to him." I've prayed this verse thousands of times. As a mother I've asked God, "Lord, HELP! I've never walked this way before, and it doesn't look like I'm going to have the opportunity to build on this experience since we have only one child, so I need help. I have no idea how to respond, discipline, or teach her—but You know. So please give me Your wisdom in this situation." I've prayed this as a wife, as a friend, as a Bible study leader. Many times and many places, my prayer has been, "Help, Lord. Teach me wisdom."

"The precepts of the LORD are right, giving joy to the heart."
What joy can come from knowing that the promises of God are trustworthy! When we have our ears open, God can speak to us with a message of love and grace that fills our hearts with joy.

Not long ago I was feeling old and fragile, unable to carry the burdens of others. Storms battered and raged not only in my life but in the lives of friends and loved ones. I needed to be strong but felt weak. I needed to help others but felt like I needed help myself. I sat in my study and said to the Lord, "Oh, Father, I'm so tired, so discouraged. I feel like I need to crawl up onto Your lap and rest there."

He answered to my heart, "Carole, you don't need to crawl up into My lap."

"Mmmm. That's true, Lord. I'm so tired I'll just ask You to lift me up and put me there."

I could almost see Him smile. "Child, I don't have to lift you up and put you there. You see, *you are already there*. In fact, I carry you close to My heart."

I thought about that a moment and then responded, "Why, then, do I feel like I'm out in the mountains caught in a thornbush, hurt and bloody?"

"Child, that's the way you may *feel* sometimes," He said gently. "But the *truth* is, I carry you close to My heart."

I prayed that my feelings would catch up to the facts. And then I read Isaiah 40:11 and 46:4, and the melody of God burst forth in my heart. Those verses say, "He tends his flock like a shepherd: He gathers the lambs in his arms and carries them close to his heart. . . . 'Even to your old age and gray hairs, I am he, I am he who will sustain you. I have made you and I will carry you; I will sustain you and I will rescue you.'"

I thought, *Of course! No matter how old I get, I'm still God's child and He carries me. He carries me close to His heart.* The truth of this verse gave me joy. I felt like laughing . . . and I did!

"The commands of the LORD are radiant, giving light to the eyes."
Sometimes—most times—it is easier to accept slander about ourselves than it is about someone we love. When children are hurt by unkindness, a mother's natural desire is to try to fix it and to strike out at the offender.

That's also true when one's husband is hurt. Mine had been. All my natural instincts wanted to lash out and retaliate. What had been said about Jack wasn't true. I felt like writing a nasty letter or going to the person and telling him off.

Did I just "happen" to be memorizing some verses in James 3 at the time? Those verses wouldn't let go of me:

> Who is wise and understanding among you? Let him show it by his good life, by deeds done in the humility that comes from wisdom. . . . But the wisdom that comes from heaven is first of all pure; then peace-loving, considerate, submissive, full of mercy and good fruit, impartial and sincere. Peacemakers who sow in peace raise a harvest of righteousness. (vv. 13,17-18)

The passage stopped me cold. The action I wanted to take wasn't peace-loving, considerate, or full of mercy and good fruit. My motive was not pure. In fact, it was vindictive. In this case, God used His Word to stop me from doing or saying anything at all. He assured me that He is the judge and will be my defender. God's Word gave me light, and it was *radiant*. The light was so bright I could see the darkness in my own heart. God's Word had exposed my sin and brought me to my knees in repentance.

The benefits from God's Word are inexhaustible, my friend, and we've only examined four of them. (Psalm 119 has an even more extensive list.) If we are deeply convinced of the worth of the Word, it will make the difference between being a lukewarm believer and one who is vitally experiencing God.

OUR RESPONSIBILITY

Don't you love the practicality of God's Word? If you and I were meeting face to face across a table, sipping a cup of coffee, I'd say to you, "Okay, we've talked about what the Word is and does. Now we'll focus on what our responsibility is. To become godly women, first we have to *know*, but then we have to *do*—and there's no way we can get around either."

In Psalm 19:11 God challenges us to do two things: to be warned and to obey. He says, "By them [God's ordinances] is your servant warned; in keeping them there is great reward." If we are warned and then obey, God promises us "great reward." We can know all the commands in the Book, but unless we keep them, they become irrelevant and useless to us. Obedience is such an important part of becoming a godly woman, we'll take a whole chapter to discuss it later in the book.

How I wish I could put my hand over yours right this minute, look you straight in the eye, and know that you are absorbing what I'm trying to convey. For unless you place the highest value on knowing and obeying God's Word, you'll not go far in your walk with Him or grow much toward becoming Christlike. You may see His wonders, but you'll never experience His heart. You may do great things, but you won't walk in His presence.

In order to know God in a deep and personal way, it's critical that you be convinced that spending time with Him—primarily through His Word—is essential. If you aren't persuaded, take the next few weeks to search and pray for this conviction. Do all the studies at the end of this chapter carefully and prayerfully. If you still aren't certain, look for other studies to do on this subject. Go to an older woman or your pastor or listen to tapes.

My heart aches when I see a woman start strong in the Christian life and then wither, much like the seed sown on shallow ground or among the rocks (Mark 4:3-9). There are a number of reasons for this, of course, but one is that she isn't convinced of how important time in God's Word is for her walk with God. As much as I'd like to, I can't give you this conviction. But I pray that *you* will pray that the Creator God of the universe, the Father who loves you beyond your comprehension, will. And that when He does, you'll walk with Him.

Making Biblical Truth Yours

Using what we learned in chapter two, let's do some verse studies on the following:

What God's Word Does
- 2 Timothy 3:16-17
- Hebrews 4:12 (Look up Ephesians 6:17 as a cross reference.)

What God's Word Is
- Proverbs 30:5-6

How Precious God's Word Is
- Jeremiah 15:16

How to Study a Psalm

And now for a big one! The longest chapter in the Bible—Psalm 119—is all about God's Word. In fact, of the 176 verses, only 5 fail to say something about God's Word. Obviously, the psalmist felt it was important—and so must we. So, for the next three weeks, let's zero in on this psalm and pray that God will put upon our hearts what He has on His.

Each day, thoughtfully and prayerfully read a section of Psalm 119. If your Bible doesn't have sections, read eight verses a day (it will take you twenty-two days to finish the psalm). Write down what the psalm says concerning:

- what the Word *is* (e.g., the Word is light: v. 105)
- what the Word *does* (e.g., the Word keeps us from sin: v. 9)
- your *responsibility* to the Word of God (e.g., my responsibility to the Word is to have it in my heart: v. 11)

Keep in mind that many words are used for the Scriptures in this psalm such as *statutes, law, precepts.*

When you've finished going through this psalm, answer these questions:

- What importance does the psalmist place upon God's Word?
- What importance should I place upon His Word?
- How does God want me to apply to my life what He is teaching me this week? (Write out a *personal application* here.)

CHAPTER FOUR

Time with the One You Love

Ways to Absorb God's Word

Jack had the red hair . . . and I had the temper. The first six years of our marriage were volatile; we clashed often. I had heard somewhere that my job was to love Jack and God's job was to make him good, but somehow I felt God needed my help! So when Jack said or did something I didn't like, my temper flared. I punished him first with cold silence, then spit out verbal venom. Our emotions spent, one of us would apologize, and the quarrel would be forgotten—until the next time. It disturbed me that our quarrels were growing more frequent, but I didn't know what to do about it.

Six years after we were married we moved to Portland, Oregon, where Jack became a youth director in a large downtown church. Three months later, he came home one evening and shouted from the front door, "Hi, honey. How's everything?" He was greeted with silence. Then, reluctantly, a cold voice answered from the kitchen, "Oh, fine." Only I wasn't fine. And by the icicles frosting my tone, he could certainly tell.

"What's the matter?" he queried, coming into the kitchen.

"Nothing," was my flat-toned response.

"I can tell something's bothering you. What is it?" he persisted.

This was exactly what I had hoped he would do. In fact, I would have been more angry if he hadn't kept asking. We had been married long enough for him to have figured one out. I can't remember what I'd been fuming about, but I do recall that whatever had been simmering on the back burner of my anger that day finally boiled over.

That was our usual pattern. However, Jack did something different that evening. Instead of lashing back at me with disgust or a quick retort, he just looked at me with love and tenderness and said quietly, "Maybe you're right. Let's pray about it together."

At first I was astonished. Then flustered. Finally, ashamed. I felt like washing myself down the drain. We did pray about it—or, rather, Jack did. I couldn't get a word past my confusion.

It was quiet at supper that evening. But finally, swallowing my pride, I gulped, "Okay, honey. What's happened to you? Why did you respond so differently than usual tonight?"

For several weeks Jack had been meeting with a young man for Bible study. They were focusing on how to apply the biblical truth they already knew. I had observed that Jack was trying to put Scripture into shoe leather in some areas he hadn't thought much about before. But this?

Jack said, "Well, I have to admit that I was a bit irritated by what you said, but a couple of weeks ago I memorized Hebrews 10:36, and just as I was going to come back at you with an angry remark, that verse came to mind. It says, 'For ye have need of patience, that, after ye have done the will of God, ye might receive the promise' (KJV). So . . . ," he paused, "I wanted to obey God."

Like a physical blow, it struck me that God was doing something real in Jack's life. I suddenly realized that if I didn't let God do something in my own heart, soon Jack and I wouldn't be on spiritual speaking terms.

Now that's not a great reason to let God do something in your life. But I've discovered that God will use *any* reason if you'll just allow Him in to do His work. That was a turnaround moment for me, one in which I was brought face to face with truth, caught a glimpse of where I'd been and where I was headed, and made a deliberate decision to change course. How grateful I am that I did.

GROWING BEYOND SPIRITUAL BOREDOM

Jack and I had attended Bible-teaching churches all our lives and had gone to Christian camps and a Christian college. I was born in a family where the Bible was not only taught but lived, and I accepted Christ as my personal Savior just prior to my teenage years. However, my growth was like a roller coaster. I'd get excited about some part of the Christian life but then dip to a low point; I'd be motivated to start spending time with God, only to have the motivation fade in a few weeks.

During Jack's four years of seminary training I learned Greek, Hebrew, and theology secondhand as I typed Jack's papers and listened to his discussions with other men in our twenty-six-foot trailer. We had tons of tremendous truth stuffed into our heads—but only a fraction of it had *gripped our souls.*

Six years later I found myself the mother of a one-year-old, the wife of an assistant pastor and youth director, and highly involved in the activities of the church. I had some expectations of what a pastor's wife was supposed to be and do, and I tried my best to live up to my own expectations.

One thing I thought a Christian—especially a pastor's wife—should do was to read a chapter of the Bible and say a prayer each morning, and I did that religiously. But one day I realized I was practicing a habit rather than meeting with the Living God. As a result, though I wouldn't have admitted it at that time, I was spiritually bored. I needed to learn how to sit at the feet of Jesus, hear Him speak, and fellowship with Him.

As Jack passed on to me what he was learning about allowing God's Word to change him, I began to spend just a few minutes—seven to ten, actually—with the Lord each morning. I'd begin by praying Psalm 119:18, "Open thou mine eyes, that I may behold wondrous things out of thy law" (KJV). I'd pray, "Lord, please give me a W.T. (wondrous thing) from Your Word today." This helped me approach the Lord with a sense of expectancy instead of a ho-hum attitude. Then I'd read the Word—not trying to get through a whole chapter but just a few verses. I read thoughtfully and prayerfully and wrote down the "wondrous things" God revealed. Then I'd pray over those things about which He was speaking to me. The few minutes grew over time, but I didn't feel guilty if I could take only five minutes to spend *quality* time with the Lord.

Friend, I'm sure your situation is different than mine was, but you may have similar feelings. You may sense that there's *got* to be more to this Christian life than you are experiencing. Your soul feels hollow. God is somewhere "out there" but not *dwelling* within you. One of the key ingredients that took my spiritual life out of the doldrums and launched me on an adventure straight up (well, with a few ups and downs!) was learning to spend time with God—not out of habit, but to meet with the Lover of my soul. This chapter is one of the most important in this book because unless we learn to spend quality time with God, it's impossible to live the Christian life in an authentic and meaningful way.

I sometimes look at something in my life and think, *That whole pattern of thought is wrong—it's screwed up, faulty, and I need to change it.* But how do I do that? I'm continuing to discover that taking in God's Word through the methods I'm going to discuss in this chapter help me make the changes that need to be made.

HOW TO ABSORB GOD'S WORD

I learned that there are a number of ways to appropriate or absorb God's Word, and I needed them all. I could *hear* the Word, *read* it, *study* it, *memorize* it, and *meditate* on it. I hope you and I will never stop growing in learning other methods, but let's explore these five for now.

Hearing the Word

In order to absorb God's Word, we first need to hear it. I'd heard hundreds of sermons but could remember only a handful because often my mind would be preoccupied: *Did I turn on the roast for Sunday dinner? What do I need to do tomorrow?* Messages, tapes, and worship services began to blow fresh air into the dusty corners of my soul as I started to really *listen* and take notes.

Before going to a meeting or listening to a tape, I began to pray that God would touch my heart with what He wanted to teach me. I'd jot down scriptures and important points and review those the next day, sometimes typing them out and keeping them in a notebook. I listened to tapes in the car or when I was fixing a meal. I was surprised to find that even with a busy schedule I could take advantage of many moments (ironing, dusting, driving, cooking) to listen to God's Word, and so can you. If this seems impossible, ask God how to manage your time in order to have more moments to sit at His feet.

Reading the Word

I determined to read through the Bible in two years, apart from what I read during my devotional time. Some people prefer to read through the Bible during their devotional time, but I yearned for that time to be a communion with the Lord when, unhurried, I could sit at His feet and tell Him I loved Him and hear Him tell me He loved me, too. If I got through only one paragraph—even one verse—in my devotional time, that was okay as long as I heard the voice of God speaking to my heart.

For Bible reading I scheduled a few minutes every day at bedtime to read several chapters. I wanted to be familiar with the entire Book because I didn't like to think of getting to heaven and having Micah ask how I liked his book and having to confess I hadn't read it! (Well, that was just one reason.) To absorb the whole scope of Scripture, I needed to know the entire panorama of God's activity throughout history.

Studying the Word

While Jack and I were in Portland, I was in a group Bible study, but often I just filled in the blanks when I did the study questions. As I prayed for a hunger to know God's Word, however, He gave me the desire to dig beneath the surface, to do more than the assignment required, to search and find exciting truths, to "let the word of Christ dwell in [me] richly" (Colossians 3:16).

I began to schedule a couple of hours during the week just for study. Some busy mothers trade off with a friend for baby-sitting and go to the library in order to do this. Women who work outside the home often schedule an evening alone. But believe me, it does have to be scheduled, or it won't get done.

Memorizing the Word

God also challenged me to do what had been so effective in changing Jack's attitude: Memorize scripture. Until our soul-changing quarrel, I had wanted no part of a Scripture memorization project. It seemed like a lot of hard work I didn't need. But a reason to do it exploded in my face when Jack responded to my anger in such a new and godly way.

I began by using the Navigators Topical Memory System and learned two or three verses and their references each week.[1] It helped to remember the "address" of a verse if I stated the reference before and after I said the verse aloud. I also discovered that the initial memorizing of a verse was a great deal easier than the retention of it!

I'd heard it said, "I used to memorize scripture [rote memory] but now *I learn it by heart*" (by applying it to my life). I like that. I began that week to "learn God's Word by heart," and it was one of the most astonishing methods God used to begin changing my character. Amazing things began to happen. Some I liked. Some hurt. Though I knew there were many areas of my personality that needed drastic surgery, the cutting process was painful. (I often say to people, "Don't memorize scripture—unless, that is, you want God to change your life." Because He will do just that as we absorb His Word into our hearts.)

One sunny afternoon, I met with a small group of women for prayer. We were drinking our second cups of coffee and discussing prayer requests.

"Well," I sighed, "I wish you'd pray for Sue. She's having trouble with her marriage. Her husband is really edgy lately and . . ." I almost strangled on the next phrase, because straight out of heaven, or so it seemed to me, God's voice intoned on my soul, "Carole (He gets very personal with me), 'A talebearer revealeth secrets: but he that is of a faithful spirit concealeth the matter'" (Proverbs 11:13, KJV).

Later, I smiled as I read 2 Timothy 3:16-17, which says that God uses His Word for teaching, for reproof, for correction, and for instruction. Without a doubt, I had just been thoroughly reproved!

One day when Lynn was about four she came bursting through the door. "Mom," she wailed, "Nancy won't play with me. She says I'm bossy and make her do things I want to and . . ." I thought I'd heard all this before, so, tuning her out, I only half-heard the remaining monologue. A pat reply had already formed in my mind. From Proverbs 18:2 God's sword poked pointedly: "Carole, 'A fool finds no pleasure in understanding but delights in airing his own opinions.' " I sank to the floor beside Lynn, my hearing set at the highest level of intensity and I *listened* . . . and *heard* her before I spoke. God continues to use this verse to remind me to listen carefully to those around me.

As God's Word was made available to my mind because I'd stored it in my heart, God changed my habits, thoughts, and desires. The times I needed power from the Word most were generally times I didn't want to look for a verse. The answer had to be readily available for God's Spirit to use in my life, sometimes like a comforting hand, at other times like a sword, and yes, sometimes even like a hammer on my head!

You may be thinking, *That all sounds wonderful, Carole, but I can't find the time to rest and put my feet up during the day. How can I make time to memorize scripture?* Good question! Glad you asked it. (You did, didn't you?)

I mentioned earlier that I listened to tapes while driving and cooking. We all have such times in our lives. I decided to put those times to good use. I began to carry Scripture verses around with me, written out on small cards, so I could go over them as I was riding in the car, ironing, vacuuming, or simply waiting. I also reviewed a few verses before I started my devotional time. It only took a minute, but those verses stuck with me throughout the day.

It's been said that we'll find time to do what we really want to do. Sometimes I've had to pray that God would give me the desire as well as the opportunity. Memorizing scripture is one method of absorbing the Word that will probably surge and abate with the seasons in your life; it has in mine. But it will be valuable beyond what you can imagine.

Meditating on the Word

While concentrating on learning and reviewing specific passages, I discovered the truth of Proverbs 23:7 (NASB): "As [a man] thinks within himself, so he is."

In many of our waking hours, our minds are of necessity occupied with routine matters. We have to give thought to our jobs, plan supper, make telephone calls, check our shopping lists. However, we spend many minutes, even hours of our day, in "mental drift." If we can give this drift direction by methodically and prayerfully dwelling on God by meditating on His Word, we can open the shutters of our thoughts to previously unknown vistas. It will help us do what Paul commands in Colossians 3:2, "*Set* your mind on the things above, not on the things that are on earth" (NASB, emphasis mine).

I don't know about you, my friend, but my thoughts are often earthly, limited, and mundane. Opening my mind to God's thoughts through meditation on Scripture passages changes the way I think . . . and thereby changes the person I am. I have found meditation to be a practical way to "look to Jesus," to keep my heart focused on Him, to not allow my thoughts to scatter in all directions, and to rest in my "hub."

I have a maverick imagination. (I sometimes wish it could be traded in for an old, steady plow horse.) My thoughts can race from a doctor's appointment or an ache in my arm to a deathbed scene in which I am the central figure. I'll be driving down the street alone in the car, tears streaming down my cheeks as I think about this dismal picture. What a waste of time—and imagination!

God gave me a mind—the ability to imagine, to reason, to think. He gave it to me so that I might honor Him. Often, however, instead of using this gift I abuse it. Knowing this, as I was driving alone one day on a two-hour trip I determined to meditate on Psalm 23 in a systematic way. I had heard of a method I could remember by the vowels *A-E-I-O-U*. That morning I experimented with this method of meditation, and I've used it many times since.

The A-E-I-O-U Meditation Method

A—Ask questions

Psalm 23 begins, "The LORD is my shepherd." I asked myself questions about that phrase such as: In what *way* is He my shepherd? (Answering that one alone took fifteen minutes.) *When* do I experience Him as my shepherd? I experience Christ most often as my shepherd in the way He guides and protects me.

That day as I meditated on Psalm 23:1, I thought about a recent time when God had guided me. A cloudburst had deluged our area just as I delivered Lynn to a church party about thirty minutes from our home. Starting back, I prayed for guidance about whether to go the way I had come (the freeway) or to go back a longer way. God seemed to indicate that the freeway should be avoided.

That was one of the scariest drives of my life. Streets were flooded. My brakes got wet, making it difficult to stop the car. Lawns were on fire from downed power lines that sent sparks crackling into the streets. Electricity was out over most of the city, making visibility even worse in the driving rain. I wondered if the car—an unreliable vehicle—would stop altogether.

Because many streets were completely blocked by flooding, I had to go miles out of my way to get home. I finally arrived, exhausted and teary, two hours later. But the scripture that sustained me on the whole trip was, "When thou passest through the waters, I will be with thee; and through the rivers, they shall not overflow thee" (Isaiah 43:2, KJV).

A news item on the front page of the paper the next day told of a woman and her twelve-year-old daughter who had attempted to use the very underpass that I would have taken onto the freeway—at the exact time I would have taken it. They had driven into twelve feet of water, and a passing motorist had to rescue them from their submerged vehicle. God, as my guiding shepherd, had cared for me in that dangerous situation.

The next phrase of Psalm 23 (KJV) reads, "I shall not want." What does this mean? Will I never want anything? In what areas have I already experienced His sufficiency?

Have you ever meditated on the beautiful fact that the more you experience Christ, the less you'll want of anything else? He has said that He is the I AM with the power to be all that I need. Do I need peace? He is my peace. Do I need security? He is my security. Whatever my need may be, He becomes the answer to that need.

On that terrifying drive through the rain, I needed several things: courage to keep driving, inner peace to keep me secure, and protection and help just to get home. God not only took care of those needs but also gave me the great assurance that He was right there in the car with me. Sometimes I know this in my head but don't feel it in my heart. That night I needed to feel His presence. And I did.

When I came to the last part of verse 4, "Thy rod and thy staff they comfort me," I was puzzled. I'd never thought about it before, but I began to contemplate how God's rod, an instrument of chastening and guidance, was a comfort. To me, it seemed like the rod would be frightening, not comforting. If God had to use His rod on me, wouldn't it be to discipline me?

One definition of meditation is "mental Bible study," and I really grappled with that one phrase. But God and I were grappling together as I prayed and thought about God's discipline. Finally the mental light switch flipped on. Yes, discipline in love *is* a comfort. What a relief it is to know that a loving Father will reach out with His rod to stop me before I fall over the cliff of disobedience. He gives me a free will to disobey, but He will do everything apart from violating that free will to keep me on the right path. That is a comforting truth.

E—Emphasize words

I took each word of Psalm 23:1 and gave emphasis to it, thinking about the importance of that particular word.

THE Lord is my shepherd—there is only one Lord.

The LORD is my shepherd—He is the Lord of lords and King of kings.

The Lord IS my shepherd—I can be positive that is exactly who He is.

The Lord is MY shepherd—how personal! He may be the shepherd to many, but I need to know He's *mine*.

The Lord is my SHEPHERD—He cares for me as His own lamb.

I—Illustrate

Illustrations can be from a number of sources. The following one came to mind from a sermon I'd heard.

A five-year-old girl was taught Psalm 23:1 by using the fingers on her left hand for each word. Touching her fingers one at a time, she'd say, "*The* (touching her thumb) *Lord* (index finger) *is* (middle) *my* (ring finger) *shepherd* (little finger)." One day she became ill and didn't recover. Her mother found her with her right hand hanging on tightly to the ring finger of her left hand. "The Lord is MY shepherd," she had been saying as she met her Shepherd face to face.

Illustrations come from Scripture, from conversations, and most frequently from our own life experiences. When we "think with God,"

He'll often bring to mind specific events to help us flesh out the verse we're meditating on.

O—Other Scriptures

As I meditated on Psalm 23, I remembered John 10:11 where Jesus said, "I am the good shepherd. The good shepherd lays down his life for the sheep." He wouldn't do anything or allow anything to come into my life that would not be right and good for me, because He is the *good* Shepherd. He also said that His sheep hear His voice (John 10:27). I took some time praying about that one, because often my ears are stuffed with self, and His voice is faint and far away.

If you are new to studying Scripture, you can use a concordance to help you with the "O" part of meditation.

U—Use

How can I use this biblical truth in my life? God had already brought so many needs to mind, it was a matter of sorting out which one He wanted me to work on first. I felt like the sheep described in a poem:

> Lord You know
> I'm such a stupid sheep.
> I worry
> about all sorts of things
> whether I'll find grazing land
> still cool water
> a fold at night
> in which I can feel safe.
> I don't.
> I only find troubles

want
loss.
I turn aside from You
to plan my rebel way.
I go astray.
I follow other shepherds
even other stupid sheep.
Then when I end up
on some dark mountain
cliffs before
wild animals behind
I start to bleat
Shepherd Shepherd
find me save me
or I die.
And You do.[2]

The two words in the poem that hit me were "I worry." You've heard of a worrywart? Well, sometimes I feel like a real toad with warts all over my body! As I thought about applying Psalm 23 in my life, I realized it promises that the great Shepherd looks out for me—even carries me. Why should I worry when He is watching over me?

That two-hour drive spent meditating was a real delight. It began a concentrated effort on my part to control my thoughts rather than letting my thoughts control me. Paul talks about "taking every thought captive to the obedience of Christ" (2 Corinthians 10:5, NASB). Meditating on Scripture helped me take my thoughts captive in obedience to Him.

One morning not long ago while sipping my cup of steaming hot chocolate as I settled down to spend time with God, it occurred to me that just as my body was absorbing that delicious drink, so must I absorb the Word of God. It needed to go down into my innermost parts, become part of me, contribute to my welfare. And that's what I pray for you: that you will absorb God's Word more deeply day by day.

Making Biblical Truth Yours

Instead of doing a study on just one verse, let's take a bigger chunk of Scripture to examine. In 2 Peter 1:3-8, we find some important principles about the promises of God and how to appropriate them.

HOW TO DO A CHAPTER STUDY

The elements of a chapter (or section) study are the same as those for a verse study, with a couple of additions. First, read the entire chapter slowly. Then, answer these questions:

What does it say?
When studying a longer portion of Scripture, you may want to outline instead of paraphrase it. For some, outlining is easier and makes it clearer as to exactly what the passage is saying.

What does it say that I don't understand?
Ask both specific questions such as, What is the "corruption that is in the world"? as well as thoughtful questions such as, Does this mean that at the moment of my rebirth, I have everything I need to be

godly? How is this possible? (Note: Consider reading other sources. For instance, if you have a good commentary on 2 Peter, read that chapter.) As you grow in this method, you may want to try to write a question for every verse.

What does it say somewhere else?

Look up other scriptures that might increase your understanding, such as 2 Corinthians 7:1. Try to find a cross-reference for each verse.

What does it say to me?

What life application of these verses does God want you to make?

Here are a few other exercises you can do to absorb more of the Word:

- Answer the same set of questions about Matthew 7:24-27. For fun, you might try to write your own illustration or parable about building on the rock.

- Compare Ephesians 6:17 and Hebrews 4:12, and write a paragraph on the analogy of the Word being a sword. How should you use a sword (skillfully, with practice, etc.)? What do you use a sword for (protection, warfare, etc.)? In what ways haven't you been using the Word as a sword, and what should you do about it?

- Finally, if you've never memorized scripture, now is the time to begin. If you have but have stopped, start again. Begin memorizing two verses each week, writing them on cards. Then review a few of them each day.

CHAPTER FIVE

Me and God

Just A-Talkin' Together

When I was three, Mother saw me walking down the street, mumbling and gesturing to an unseen companion. When she asked me what I was doing, I replied, "Oh. Me and God. We was just a-talkin' together."

Mother thought that was a great definition of prayer. I agree.

But as I grew older, I lost my childlike faith and the habit of conversing with God constantly. In my late twenties I had to enter the school of prayer in earnest. I had a lot of lessons to learn.

LESSON #1: NOTHING IS TOO SMALL TO PRAY ABOUT

The first time I recall getting a glimmer of how much God was interested in the details of my life was a few weeks after we moved to Portland, Oregon. I had to take a bus to a doctor's appointment, but as I reached the corner, I saw the bus disappearing down the street.

I looked after it, feeling helpless and frustrated, irritated with the baby-sitter who had been late and put out with the doctor two transfers away who waited for no one and charged the patient if an appointment was missed. I even felt thwarted by the bus driver who kept that dumb bus on time.

Then I thought, *Wait a minute! I wonder if God is interested in my getting to that doctor on time. Is this something I can pray about? Well, it can't hurt to try.*

At that time I was just beginning to realize that God wanted to be involved in the "dailies" of my life and that He was concerned with every circumstance and detail. But I was still unsure of my ground. I didn't know how I could ask for God's help for my mundane problems when so many people had such gigantic needs. Mine seemed trivial. I guess I thought that God had a priority list of prayers to answer and my requests were sure to be on the bottom.

But a study of Psalm 139 revolutionized my view of prayer. I discovered that God knows every thought I am thinking. He even knows when I sit down and when I stand up! He knew what my nose and mouth and arms and legs were going to look like...before I was conceived. I realized nothing was too little to ask him about—or too big. He might just be *waiting* for me to ask.

So on that street corner I bowed my head (at this point in my life I didn't think I could pray with my eyes open) and asked the Lord to help me get to the doctor's office on time. I'm not sure how I expected God to answer that prayer, but perhaps He'd hurry along the next bus, which wasn't due for twenty minutes, so I could make the proper transfers.

Instead, as I opened my eyes, a car pulled alongside the curb, and a feminine voice greeted me. "Hi, Carole," she said. "Where are you headed?" She was one of the few people I knew in all of Portland. When I told her where I was going, she responded, "I'm driving to within a block of there. Hop in."

I couldn't quite believe this wasn't simply a coincidence, so I said to my friend, "I suppose you go this way all the time?"

She answered, "No, this is the first time I've gone this way in a year."

A giant crack appeared in my dam of doubt, and my faith, a mere trickle at first, began to flow more freely. God, the great God of the universe, was personally interested in the tiniest happenings of my life.

In the weeks that followed I reflected on why God said to "ask...ask...ask. I want you to ask. I beg you to ask. Please ask." He wants us to ask because He won't violate our wills by forcing things on us that we don't care to request of Him.

That year I heard a man speak who had walked with God for many years. He told of having a dream in which God showed him a vast storehouse in heaven filled with wrapped packages. As they explored this warehouse, Jim spied a small package that had his name on it with a date of some years before.

"What's that?" Jim asked.

"Oh, that is pabulum," the Lord replied. "I had it all packaged and ready to send...but you didn't ask Me." And Jim remembered that on that date he and his wife had desperately needed pabulum for their baby but hadn't had money to buy it.

Down the aisle, Jim spotted another larger package with a date and his name written on it.

"What's that?" asked Jim.

"Oh, that's folding chairs. I had them all wrapped and ready to send. But you didn't ask Me." And Jim remembered the time when they'd had servicemen over every week who had to sit on the floor because Jim had no folding chairs to offer them.

Jim's dream challenged me deeply. How many packages were in

God's storehouse for me—all wrapped up and ready to send—but *I hadn't asked for them?* I determined to start asking. When I began to talk to God about the little things in my life, my days took on another dimension, a new excitement. To ask for specific things and see Him answer in specific ways was a thrill because I learned more of the Father-heart of God and how He cares for me.

Another reason we are to ask is because He commands it. We ask simply because He said to. Our Father—loving us more than we can comprehend—longs to be involved with us, yearns to fill to overflowing every crevice and corner of our lives. ("Overflow" and "overflowing" are used a number of times in Scripture—look them up.)

LESSON #2: GOD ALWAYS ANSWERS PRAYER

A year later Jack and I had an opportunity for our faith to grow and flex its weak muscles in a way we wouldn't have chosen but was, perhaps, the most concrete way we could have experienced God's direct provision.

Neither Jack nor I had a great deal of money sense at that time. When we had money, we spent it, and sometimes even if we didn't have it, we spent it. We had moved from a little three-room apartment, furnished with borrowed furniture, to a large older home. We bought some furniture on credit. About the same time our car gave out and had to be traded in on a new one, also purchased on monthly installments. We woke up one day to the fact that our salary simply wasn't covering our monthly bills. We began to put off one credit payment to meet another, and even then we barely made it through each month.

We were convicted by the scripture that says, "Owe nothing to anyone" (Romans 13:8, NASB). God began to show us that our lifestyle wasn't honoring Him. Our mess was of our own making. (It's terrible when you can't blame anyone else, isn't it?) So we asked God's forgiveness and told Him we really wanted to learn from our failure and would do whatever He wanted. We were beginning to see we needed to ask God about what to do and wait for His answer instead of taking matters into our own hands.

While we prayed, we talked about our options. We considered selling everything but realized we could get only a fraction of what we needed and would still be in debt. We prayed about my going back to work until all our bills were paid in full. Lynn was two, old enough for nursery school. But as we searched the Word, God indicated very clearly that for this period I was to be one of those "workers at home" (Titus 2:5, NASB). What, then?

As we sought God's will, he put it on both Jack's and my heart (independently from each other so we were sure it was from Him) to pay all our bills at the beginning of the month. On installment loans we were to pay *more* than was due if we were able, and we were to trust Him for everything the rest of the month. Payday was once a month, on the first, which meant that by the fifth we would often be without any funds at all.

This terrified me. I knew verses like "My God shall supply all your needs" (Philippians 4:19, NASB), and food is definitely a need. But I was afraid God wouldn't supply; and if He didn't, our belief, both in our ability to know His will for us in a given situation as well as in His promises, could erode, making our schooling, our work in the ministry, and our purpose in life invalid and futile.

A. W. Tozer said:

> We can prove our faith by our committal to it, and in no
> other way. . . . Pseudo faith always arranges a way out to
> serve in case God fails it. . . . For true faith it is either God
> or total collapse. . . . The man of pseudo faith will fight
> for his verbal creed but refuse flatly to allow himself to get
> into a predicament where his future must depend upon
> that creed being true.[1]

"Pseudo faith always arranges a way out." I wondered if I had the faith to put myself out on a limb with God where so much hinged on whether or not God would do what we believed He had told us. It's a scary thing to be out on that limb. Being out there means we take risks: We put ourselves in a perilous place and trust God to keep the limb from breaking—no matter what! It means trusting that we are obeying Him and following His lead while acknowledging that we may not know His mind and therefore can't predict in this life what the outcome will be.

Now don't misunderstand me here. There have been a few incidents where I thought God was saying one thing and He was saying something else entirely. At one point I was positive that God was promising another child—and then out of the blue we were offered a child to adopt. I was devastated when God gave us no peace about going ahead with the adoption and couldn't understand what in the world was going on.

God's ways are not our ways; of that we can be sure. But over and over Jack and I have experienced God's giving us concrete direction in uncertain situations, and we often claim Psalm 32:8 where God said, "I will instruct you and teach you in the way you should go; I will counsel you and watch over you." In the few times God didn't seem to direct us, I couldn't doubt His Word because in a multitude of other times He had demonstrated that He *did* direct us. I realized I wouldn't throw out a recipe that I had used to make wonderful bread a hundred times when it failed to come out right once. I wouldn't blame the recipe; I had somehow messed up the ingredients. God never fails, even when it looks to me as if He has. But in those early days of shaky faith and wobbly knees, I think God knew we needed some unusual evidences of His faithfulness.

We prayed. We covenanted with God that we would tell no one what we were doing. We knew that one phone call would bring help from our parents. A hint might bring money from friends. For six months we lived not knowing if we would have money for the next meal. And yet we always had food to eat—for every meal.

Incredible things happened. An aunt I had never heard from before or since sent a Valentine's Day card with five dollars enclosed. Jack found a wallet with sixty dollars in it and, on returning it, was rewarded with ten dollars. (The owner was surprised that any money was left in it at all.) One day we found bags of groceries on our back porch.

During that time Jack had an emergency appendectomy. We had no insurance. The same day the hospital bill came, we received a refund on our income tax that paid it in full. The day the doctor's bill arrived, three different men in the church, not knowing our circumstances, gave enough money to cover the exact amount.

We developed convictions during those months. One was that if God brought in food for the day, we wouldn't try to make it stretch for three. We remembered that the manna God rained down on His people in the wilderness was good only for one day. So we would eat the food and pray for the next day's supply.

One week we were especially tested as we ate pancakes for several days in a row. We did have milk delivered and a giant supply of pancake mix! But for the rest of the time, we ate as we would normally have done, often having groups of young people into our home. Sometimes we felt like the widow feeding Elijah (1 Kings 17:10-15), wondering if there would be "oil in the jug," but we were never short of food to serve.

Each month our faith grew a bit stronger. God had provided.

LESSON #3: FAITH GROWS WHEN WE KEEP A RECORD OF RESULTS

God always answers prayer. At times the answer is no, and a very firm no at that. Other times God says, "Wait awhile. The time is not right." No matter what His answer, our faith can be strengthened by His faithfulness.

Some of you, like me, feel discombobulated concerning your prayer life. In the past often people would ask me to pray about something and I'd say, "Sure, I'll pray." Later, they would thank me for praying, and I would realize I'd not only forgotten to pray but I'd forgotten what they'd ask me to pray *about*. This was not merely embarrassing; I realized that I'd *lied* when I said I would pray. I was grateful to get some tips from Marion, the woman who discipled me, on how to pray for the people and situations that were important to me.

I started a prayer notebook. First, I wrote down everything I felt the need to pray about: current personal needs, friends I'd promised to pray for, our church, our nation. The list looked horrendous! I was glad there was a second step.

I divided the list into two separate kinds of requests. One page was for current and immediate needs ("Immediate Prayer Requests") that required specific answers within a certain period of time: people who were ill, a financial crisis, wisdom for an important pending decision. I wrote these requests on the left side of the paper, put a line down the middle, and dated the request. At the top of the right-hand side I wrote "Answer." (I've included what these pages looked like in the studies at the end of this chapter.)

I began with a rather doubtful attitude, but my skepticism quickly eroded as answers began to fill the pages. I recorded God's "no" and "wait" responses as well as His "yes's." In retrospect, I have sometimes thanked Him more for His "no's" than His "yes's" as I've seen His wisdom in delivering me from some things I thought were "musts."

Sometimes when I had to wait a long time for an answer that was especially important to me, I tended to think, *Well, God isn't answering my prayers anymore.* Then I'd wonder if He ever had. (Sometimes my memory gets rather short.) With those lists before me, however, I discovered I couldn't doubt God was meeting my needs in exciting ways—even when those "wait" or "no" answers appeared frequently on my list. When a page was full but the answers to some of the requests were pending, I put a *T* for "transfer" on the Answer side and started a new page.

It took only a few months to convince me of the value of writing down my prayer requests and God's answers. When the enemy tempted me to think that something was mere coincidence, all I had to do was look over page after page of specific answers, and Satan had to close his mouth.

The second page was for people for whom I wanted to pray regularly—family, friends, church members, missionaries, national leaders—but didn't know of any urgent or specific request to record. I put an equal number of these "Permanent Prayer Requests" under each of the six days of the week, leaving Sunday free. Later, I added a page of requests specifically for my husband and one page for my daughter.

If you begin keeping a prayer notebook, I suggest you read over the pages on New Year's Day each year. Reflecting on God's faithfulness is a wonderful way to begin the new year!

LESSON #4: WE SHOULD PRAY THAT GOD WILL TEACH US WHAT TO PRAY

One day it occurred to me that if I used just a fraction of the time I spent washing, ironing, and cooking for Jack *praying* for him, the investment might bring great dividends. My application for that week was to spend ten minutes a day praying just for Jack. I didn't think ten minutes would bankrupt my day.

I looked at my watch as I began. I prayed and prayed. When I glanced at my watch again, one minute had elapsed! I started again and found myself praying for the people he was meeting, his work, and various other things. But my covenant had been to pray for *Jack*, not things related to him.

That day I had to pray to learn what to pray about. Like the disciples of old, I said, "Father, teach me to pray! I thought I knew something about prayer, but I can't seem to pray for my husband for two minutes. Please help me."

I started again…and I found myself praying about things I hadn't ever thought to think about, let alone pray about. I began to pray certain passages of Scripture for him such as Colossians 1:9-12, that Jack would be filled with the knowledge of God's will "through all spiritual wisdom and understanding"; that he would live a life worthy of the Lord and please Him in every way; that he would bear "fruit in every good work, growing in the knowledge of God"; and that he'd be "strengthened with all power according to God's glorious might" so that he would have great endurance and patience and give God thanks joyfully. (Now *that's* a prayer to pray for loved ones, isn't it?) As God brought things to mind for Jack, I'd jot them down on the prayer page reserved for him. I didn't tell Jack what I was doing, but he began asking me to pray things for him that he hadn't ever mentioned before.

Most of us spend considerable hours thinking about the advice we'd like to give our husbands or loved ones. Some of us give it. What greater things would be accomplished in their lives if we would spend at least an equal amount of time in prayer for them.

LESSON #5: GOD DELIGHTS TO DELIGHT US

Did you know that the delight of God's heart is to delight His children? God has promised not only to meet our needs but to delight us as well. When I discovered this one, it boggled my mind! David said, "The LORD be magnified, who delights in the prosperity of His servant" (Psalm 35:27, NASB). God delights to delight me!

I heard somewhere that "prayer is conversation between two people who love each other," and it's true. When we love someone deeply, we want to share everything with them—thoughts, wishes, desires, dreams, hurts, and *delights*—from a view of the Grand Canyon to the startling blue of a forget-me-not. In an intimate relationship, mutual sharing, transparency of soul, and opening up our hearts and minds to the other is crucial. And that's exactly what God desires with us. If we talk to Him only about our needs, we leave Him out of vast areas of our lives. We know from Scripture that God is the giver of all good things, but if we don't ask, how are we going to know that it is God who is pouring forth His love in giving us those great and wonderful things?

When I began to realize that God delights to delight me and be intimately involved in my life, two other lists in my prayer notebook developed: a "Blessing List" and a "Bonus List."

Blessing List

If you and I could begin to fathom all the things God provides for us each day, we would overflow with thanksgiving. However, often we don't even think about—let alone feel grateful for—the gifts of having clean air to breathe, legs that don't buckle when we walk, and enough food on the table. And alongside the blessings we take for granted are the countless times we pray a quick "arrow" prayer, God answers, and we forget even to thank Him.

God began to get my attention concerning this as throughout the day I would ask Him for small, everyday needs such as time to open up in Jack's schedule so we could have a few minutes to chat, safety as I drove the freeway, a parking place close to the entrance to the post office, wisdom with a difficult phone call, finding something that was lost. Often God would answer, "Yes!" but not only didn't I say, "Thank You," I'd also forget all about those answers the next day. So it was an adventure to begin to keep a little diary of those blessings at the end of each day and review them at the end of the week. I was amazed at what I saw. Most of these things weren't "needs" such as I put on my prayer pages but small requests I made during the day. One week I wrote 121 items on my Blessing List!

Bonus List

But there's more. I also started keeping a list of the "it-sure-would-be-nice-to-have" things that I talk to God about. James tells us that "you do not have because you do not ask" (James 4:2, NASB). He goes on to say that "you ask and do not receive, because you ask with wrong motives, so that you may spend it on your pleasures" (4:3, NASB). God knows much better than I do what might make me selfish and become sin in my life, so as I put items on my Bonus List, I am careful to say, "If it wouldn't be good for me to have, Lord, I don't want it. But if it would delight Your heart to delight *my* heart in this way, I would be most grateful."

I've had big things, little things, silly and not-so-silly things on my Bonus List over the years. One summer when Lynn was ten, we traveled to the West Coast and into Canada and found some of the most beautiful scenery in the world driving the sixty miles from Banff to Jasper National Park. All three of us enjoyed the magnificent views. But Lynn and I especially wanted to see some wild animals. Now, we didn't *need* to see wild animals. We just *wanted* to see them. We decided to ask God about this.

You wouldn't believe the wild animals we saw! It took us all day to travel that sixty miles because we had to stop and take pictures at every bend in the road. We saw bear, deer, elk, moose, and mountain goats. There was even a doe and her fawn walking down the main street in the town of Jasper.

The next day on the ride back I thought, *I wonder if people just naturally see a lot of wild animals up here in the summer. Could it be a coincidence?* (You can see I still needed a lot of growing in faith.) So we didn't pray to see any wild animals on the way back—and *we didn't see one*.

I have prayed for big things such as the opportunity to travel overseas. Two years after I recorded this desire on my Bonus List, we were on our way around the world. The trip expanded my horizons and deepened my concern for missionaries and nations. The money for the trip was provided in such a way that I had no doubt it was from a God who delights to give to His children.

I have prayed for landscaping and shoes and new coats. One winter a number of years ago, I found myself with a threadbare but serviceable coat. I didn't really like that coat, but I couldn't honestly say I needed a new one. So I put a new coat on the Bonus List in my prayer notebook and asked God that if it would please Him, I would surely appreciate a new coat. Within four days I was given *three* coats! I had the fun of giving away two to friends who were in greater need than I was. That was a bonus on the bonus.

My love for God has grown as I've realized how graciously He gives me the "desires of my heart." He isn't a grudging giver. He *wants* to thrill my heart with His goodness.

LESSON #6: LISTENING TO GOD IS A BIG PART OF PRAYER

While probably 98 percent of the time (I tend to make up statistics!), God speaks to me through Scripture, there have been critical times when He has spoken distinctly to my heart while I'm praying. He will, that is, if I keep quiet long enough to let Him.

The first time I began to get a glimmer of how God speaks directly to my heart was in a crisis situation. It had been one of *those* months. It seemed the whole world had fallen in on top of me and I was lying amidst the rubble. Two very precious friends were in the hospital with emotional illnesses; one showed up at our home disoriented and desperate and had to be hospitalized that very day. A flood in our lower level (where our bedroom was) had left us with much repair and redecorating to be done, and the whole house was torn up for two months.

One afternoon Jack told me that an emotionally distraught young man was coming over to talk with him. He wanted the house to be quiet as he met with this person in the living room. That meant I had to sit by the phone to grab it on the first hint of a ring.

I went down into our rugless, messy bedroom and collapsed on the cement floor by the bed (right beside the telephone) and buried my face in my hands. There I cried and prayed. Several years before, I had memorized Psalm 62:8 (NASB), which says, "Trust in [the Lord] at all times, O people; pour out your heart before Him; God is a refuge for us." In my most depressed and anxious moments, I would go to God and tell Him all about it—every little detail, every complaint, every heartache. What a comfort it is to take all to the God who listens with compassion and can be trusted not only to be compassionate but who is able to *do* something about it.

That day I told Him all my problems, beginning with A and going way past Z. Then I said, "Lord, I've had it! I've had it up to here. I just can't take any more. I feel like going away, running off, and hiding." I ran out of words but stayed on my knees, silent before Him. I'm so glad I waited.

I guess I thought He might bring to my mind that I was to "give thanks in everything." But He didn't do that. Or perhaps He would tell me to count my blessings, because I really had a great many even though I wasn't appreciating them at the moment. But He didn't tell me that either. Instead, very quietly but distinctly, God impressed on my heart two words: "Go ahead."

I said audibly, "I beg Your pardon, Lord?" I was new at listening as I prayed and thought I must be putting words into my own mind because that answer didn't make any sense to me. But again, the firm directive came: "Go ahead and hide. Hide...in me."

Suddenly all the psalmist's pleas for God to "hide me" rushed into my mind. I had never thought about what that really meant...to hide in God. Quickly I grabbed a Bible concordance and began looking up the verses that mention God as our hiding place. And what a joy it was! All my frustrations and cares were swept up and discarded as God picked me up from the rubble of my self-pity and hid me in the Rock of Ages.

The house didn't get cleaned the next week. And the people I was so concerned about didn't suddenly get well. In fact, all the problems I had been having stayed right there with me. But throughout the whole week, I hid in God. As I interacted with those around me, I thought, *You may see me, but you can't touch me, because I'm hiding this week*—and I really was. It was as though a wall of protection surrounded me emotionally and nothing touched the "inner me" all that week. I learned a little about what it meant that God was literally a shelter, a cleft, a hiding place for my weary heart and soul.

The next week God said, "Okay, Carole, you've been hiding long enough. I've healed your frayed emotional nerve endings. Time for you to come out and fight in the battle now." And I was strengthened and refreshed to do just that.

Conversation is two-way, or it isn't conversation at all. Conversation includes both talking and listening. So how do you learn to listen to God?

Someone has said that listening is done with one's mouth firmly shut! So punctuate talking with God with periods of silence, making concentrated effort to keep your mind focused on what you're praying about but opening your mind to His thoughts. When a thought impresses itself upon your mind, take note. Sometimes that thought will be so unlike anything you'd think up yourself, you'll have no doubt it's from God; other times, you won't be so sure. Don't worry about that. God's whispers will always line up with Scripture. He won't go against principles in His own Word—He is the same yesterday, today, and forever (Hebrews 13:8)—so you don't have to worry that the thought might be from the Enemy.

Most often God speaks words of comfort and assurance to us, but if He gives us a command or some unusual direction, we can pray for a verse of Scripture to confirm it. In extremely critical situations, I've asked for two or three passages that tell me the same thing that I feel He has said so I can be absolutely sure. Remember Gideon in the book of Judges, who asked for two opposite signs or miracles to confirm what God had already told him to do? God didn't get angry at Gideon for asking for those confirmations. He understood Gideon's human doubts so well.

CONTINUING IN THE SCHOOL OF PRAYER

You and I may quit the school of prayer, but we'll never finish. There are always new lessons to learn. Let's pray we'll learn them well.

Jeremiah said, "The LORD'S lovingkindnesses indeed never cease, for His compassions never fail. They are new every morning" (Lamentations 3:22-23, NASB). *New every morning.* What new thing is He doing for you today? For me? Often we experience little of Him because we don't *ask*.

And Jesus said to ask: "Ask, and you will receive, that your joy may be made full" (John 16:24, NASB).

Making Biblical Truth Yours

As I've said, prayer is conversation between two people who love each other. It is a critical ingredient of our love relationship with God.

Let's start off with some *verse studies* on prayer:

- *God's promise:* John 14:13-14
- *God's assurance:* John 15:7
- *God's command that we ask:* John 16:24
- *God's condition:* 1 John 3:21-23

HOW TO DO A CHARACTER STUDY

Now, let's learn how to do another type of study—the study of a person in the Bible. With some biblical characters, such as David or Peter, you would have too much material to cover, so the study would need to be broken into segments such as David's heart toward God or a contrast of Peter's character before and after the resurrection. But generally, in doing a character study, a person is chosen about whom not quite so much is written and who exemplifies the subject chosen for study.

Because we are studying prayer, let's look at a woman in the Old Testament, Hannah, who pled with God about a desperate part of her life. Here is how to do a character study:

1. *Read the portions of Scripture dealing with the person,* taking notes as you read. In this case you'd read 1 Samuel 1–2:10.

2. *Summarize in a brief page* the facts about that person. These can be "fact-facts" (for example, Hannah was one of two wives of Elkanah and had no children, etc.) or your interpretation of those facts (for example, It was a terrible disgrace in those days for a woman to be barren, and Hannah must have felt awful).

3. In a paragraph, sketch what you consider to be *the outstanding quality* of the person's life and why (for example, Hannah had great determination to keep on praying year after year, or, To me, the outstanding quality of Hannah's life was her faithfulness in keeping her word after Samuel was born).

4. Jot down any *questions* that come to mind.

5. Pray about and then write down a *personal application* (see page 25). When I studied Hannah, God spoke to me about being persistent and fervent in my praying. My application was to pray *out loud* three mornings a week for a month.

START A PRAYER NOTEBOOK

Now is the time for you to begin keeping the prayer notebook I've described in this chapter. Make it loose-leaf so you'll be able to add to it. The following are some of the pages you might have in your notebook:

Immediate Prayer Requests

REQUEST	ANSWERS
1. Ann's surgery: for healing (January)	February: She came through well.
2. Wisdom to accompany Jack on trip (January)	February: God said no.
3. Sale of Fred's home (August)	Still waiting.
4.	

Permanent Prayer Requests

MONDAY:

Relatives (requests will change periodically)

TUESDAY:

Needs in the church

WEDNESDAY:

Missionaries (names, places, needs)

THURSDAY:

Friends

FRIDAY:

Friends

SATURDAY:

The country, government officials, etc.

Blessing List

    Tom spared from injuries in car accident Saturday

    Wonderful worship service Sunday

    The ability to see and smell the lilacs

    The joy and laughter of special times with family

Bonus List

    Balloon ride

    Organ lessons

    For hummingbirds to discover our feeder

    For good weather the two days we're in the Caribou Mountains

CHAPTER SIX

Whatever Happened to Obedience?

Taking God Seriously

*S*ome six hundred women crowded into the auditorium, eager to hear the prominent Christian speaker. I was among them.

Her address was well presented, warm, and powerful. "What will you be remembered for fifty years from now?" she challenged us. I, perhaps along with most of the audience, silently answered her, *To be honest, probably nothing.*

Her well-intentioned point was that doing small faithful acts now can grow into big things that will be remembered after we die. She cited the example of Henrietta Mears, who saw a need for grade-appropriate Sunday school materials. Miss Mears obeyed God's nudge to write the Sunday school materials she envisioned, and when she couldn't interest a publisher, she printed the material herself, and Gospel Light Publishing House was born.

I frowned as I thought, *But we're a pretty ordinary group of women sitting here. Not too many Henrietta Mearses among us. Where does that leave us unexceptional people?*

As I pondered the speaker's question, shadows clouded my mood. But suddenly I brightened as I thought, *Wait! She's asking us the wrong question! Does it really matter if anyone remembers me for something fifty years from now? To be remembered would be nice, but unnecessary. What is vital is that I wholeheartedly, all-out, 100 percent obey God today, this hour, this minute.*

When I stand before God, His question won't be, "What have you done that people remember?" Rather, He'll ask, "What have you done with My Son, Jesus?" Life isn't about pleasing people. It's about pleasing God. And what pleases Him most? True obedience. (I started to say "simple obedience" but then realized there wasn't anything simple about it!)

If you have children, you know how difficult it is to train a child to obey, but you also realize how critical it is. I remember hearing about a mother whose small son walked a few feet ahead of her in their hike through the desert. Suddenly the mother yelled, "Don't move!" The boy froze in his tracks as a giant rattler uncoiled and slithered away. Many children would have paid scant attention and kept right on walking. Others would have looked at their mother and asked, "Why shouldn't I?" This boy was saved because he *obeyed*.

The value God puts on obedience is incalculable. To Him, obedience is better than any sacrifice we can offer (1 Samuel 15:22). Example after example in Scripture demonstrates that God rewards obedience and punishes disobedience, but today we hear more sermons on God's love than we do on obedience. In our age of permissiveness and challenge of authority, many of us need to change our thought patterns concerning obedience. So let's talk about the importance of obeying God and what it means in your life and mine.

"SELL EVERYTHING YOU HAVE
AND FOLLOW ME"

I remember a young woman who asked for some time with me after I'd spoken to a group on the subject of obeying God. She was young, pretty, and married just six months to a law student she had met in college. Both she and her husband had become Christians at the university and had received extensive premarital counseling. Her husband was so busy now, however, with both graduate school and work that there wasn't a lot of time to talk or have fun anymore.

Then she told me about a man she worked with: handsome, attentive, attracted to her. They enjoyed talking, laughing, and working together and had a lot in common. She found herself thinking it was more enjoyable to be with him than with her husband. There hadn't been anything physical—just a flirtation—but she was a bit concerned where it was going. What should she do?

After exploring the subject a bit further, I said, "You may have to quit your job." She looked as though a bag full of rattlesnakes had been thrown in her lap. "Quit my job?" she gasped. "But it's a good job. I like it. In today's economy, I'd never be able to find one that pays nearly as well." A frown made furrows between her eyes as she twisted a tissue into a small ball.

I continued, "There are some things the Bible says we are to turn and run from—to *flee*. We aren't to fight an internal battle or to flirt or play with these things; we're told to *get away!* These things include sexual immorality (1 Corinthians 6:18), idolatry (1 Corinthians 10:14), loving money (1 Timothy 6:10), and the evil desires of youth (2 Timothy 2:22). I know that's not easy, but at times God asks us to make hard decisions. This may be one of them for you."

She was shaking her head as she left my room, and I was reminded of the rich man who went away sorrowful because the Lord Jesus had said, "Go, sell everything you have. . . . Then come, follow me" (Mark 10:21). My heart whispered, *Whatever happened to obedience?*

PARTIAL OBEDIENCE EQUALS NO OBEDIENCE

Friend, God puts a premium on obedience. When He talks about it, he doesn't pull any punches. Over and over during Christ's final discourse with His disciples before He was crucified, He drummed in the connection between love and obedience, stating, "If you love me, you will obey what I command" (John 14:15); "Whoever has my commands and obeys them, he is the one who loves me" (John 14:21); "You are my friends if you do what I command" (John 15:14).

Hannah Whitall Smith in her classic *The Christian's Secret of a Happy Life* gives this illustration:

> I was once trying to explain to a physician who had charge of a large hospital the necessity and meaning of consecration, but he seemed unable to understand. At last I said to him, "Suppose, in going your rounds among your patients, you should meet with one man who entreated you earnestly to take his case under your especial care in order to cure him, but who should at the same time refuse to tell you all his symptoms or to take all your prescribed remedies and should say to you, 'I am quite willing to follow your directions as to certain things, be-

cause they commend themselves to my mind as good, but in other matters I prefer judging for myself, and following my own directions.' What would you do in such a case?" I asked.

"Do!" he replied with indignation. "Do! I would soon leave such a man as that to his own care. For, of course," he added, "I could do nothing for him unless he would put his whole case into my hands without any reserves, and would obey my directions implicitly."

"It is necessary, then," I said, "for doctors to be obeyed if they are to have any chance to cure their patient?"

"Implicitly obeyed," was his emphatic reply.

"And that is consecration," I continued. "God must have the whole case put into His hands without any reserves, and His directions must be implicitly followed."

"I see it," he exclaimed, "I see it! And I will do it. God shall have his own way with me from henceforth."[1]

Unlike this wise gentlemen, many of us take lightly what God takes seriously. We shrug off God's commands as though they were dust instead of dynamite, not realizing that disobeying them has consequences so explosive they can shatter our Christian walk. We offer only a partial obedience, one that suits our own agenda. Perhaps that's because, without even realizing it, we have bought into what the world is selling.

WE'VE BEEN DUPED

Perhaps an analogy will help.

I cup spring's first burst of sunshine in my hand. I note the deep yellow center and the hundreds of bright petals so perfectly formed and I think, *Why do they call this dandelion a weed?*

A week later the yard is a velvet yellow carpet, and as I admire the lavish explosion of color I think again, *They're lovely flowers—not weeds!*

But some days after, I note that yellow has turned to white and thousands of seeds form a cloud in the wind. Another week goes by, and the ragged edges of dandelion leaves turn the yard into poor urchin's clothes and make mowing necessary. But the leaves of the dandelions grow more rapidly than the grass, so in less than twenty-four hours the lawn looks unmowed, uneven, and ugly.

Were I to leave my lawn untended, the dandelions would take over completely, crowding out the grass and leaving bare spots of dirt between the clumps of leaves. When I try to rid the lawn of the weeds, I discover that dandelions are tenacious! Pulling out the weed above the ground won't do it; the roots are deep and strong, and a deter-mined effort with a trowel or weed-killer is needed to eliminate the pesky things.

No wonder dandelions are called weeds.

We live in a dandelion society where weeds are rapidly taking over. Most of us have not only stopped fighting the takeover, but we have allowed spiritual dandelions to take root in our hearts. Society thinks the bare dirt and pollen are natural, normal, and acceptable. People have even changed the name of the weeds. A person isn't promiscuous but "sexually active"; not a prostitute but a "lady of the night"; not a homosexual but "gay" with an "alternate lifestyle." Women don't have abortions or kill babies but are "pro-choice" and "eliminate a bit of fetal matter" in order to have control over their own bodies. To the world, homosexuality isn't sin; intolerance of the lifestyle is. Adultery isn't the problem; it's the bigotry of those who don't understand. Judging someone else's behavior—no matter how deviant or abhorrent that behavior may be—is considered the ultimate evil.

I'm afraid that we Christians have started to filter the Word of God through our cultural glasses instead of filtering our culture through the Word of God. We have allowed people, rather than God, to define sin, evil, and judgment. I've slowly been brainwashed, too. Words on TV that shocked me five years ago barely register today. If a movie has only one or two erotic scenes, a few swear words, and only a couple of graphic murders, I'm liable to remember it as a fairly clean story. Slowly, subtly, but very surely, I am in danger of accepting the unacceptable. Oh, I come up with excuses: "I've got to live in the world, know what's going on, adjust." True. Perhaps I do need to be aware of the garbage out there. But if I'm not careful, not only do I begin eating it, but I become so used to it I don't even know it's garbage I'm eating.

Sometimes I need to check myself as to whether I am becoming indifferent to sin. In the past few months I've heard of two people having an affair right under the noses of their respective spouses. I know a married missionary to India who brought his mistress to the field. I've listened to a woman, once widowed, once divorced, telling me tearfully, "I go out with men and just can't help going to bed with them. I just can't *live* without sex."

These people all claimed to be Christians, but they allowed the dandelions of sin to take root in their lives. Oh, that we would have the determination to pull those weeds out by the roots no matter the cost!

Make no mistake: God hates sin. Giving sinful behavior a new name won't change the fact that it is sinful. God wouldn't allow his servant Moses into the Promised Land because of a single lapse in his life. Sin always has been and always will be *anything* that disregards God's laws. God's Word thunders uncompromisingly, "Get rid of all bitterness . . . and anger" (Ephesians 4:31). In other words, all sin. God and His Word stand forever the same.

THE BEAUTY OF OBEDIENCE

Listen, my friend. Satan is out to destroy you and me. He entices us into sin, slowly and subtly, sucking us in further and further until we are stuck up to our necks in life-threatening quicksand.

In the workplace we become desensitized to bad language, foul jokes, cheating, lying, and office affairs. As we work with attractive men, it's easy to start fantasizing and flirting and to begin friendships we label as "professional" and "platonic." We fail to put necessary guards around our hearts and lives. I can't tell you how many times I've heard the words, "I didn't mean for it to happen!"

In the midst of busy, stressful days, it's easy to let our communion time with God slip away. When we do, we lose not only our sensitivity to God's small warning voice but the desire to obey Him. Does it seem to you that the battle gets more fierce every day? How we need an ever-stronger resolve to follow God at all costs!

One woman I met with was positive she could reestablish a relationship with a former boyfriend—one she'd lived with before she was married—on a purely platonic basis. I was just as sure she couldn't. "It would be dangerous, like playing with dynamite," I said. "While it might never ignite, the danger isn't worth the risk."

"Oh, Carole," she said. "You're so straight!" She used that word every time we had a different outlook on a subject concerning obedience to God's Word. The next time she said, "Oh, Carole, you're so straight," I replied, "You know, that may be true, but I think what you're calling 'straight,' I'm calling 'obedience.'"

She blinked, swallowed, and then slowly replied, "You know, I think you're right."

We've laughed about it since. I guess I shouldn't have been surprised that a child of the sixties who didn't want to be confined by rules would label "my" rules as straight. But when she understood they weren't *my rules* but *God's commandments*, her attitude and life changed.

If we want to be godly, we can't play games with obedience. So, friend, please stop a moment to ask the Father to speak deeply to your heart as you consider the rest of this chapter. It is vital!

THE BENEFITS OF OBEDIENCE

There are many reasons for taking God seriously, for obeying His Word, for standing mentally at attention and, as He gives us a command, responding, "Yes, SIR!"

Obedience Protects Us

Obeying God will not only keep our lives pure but will also keep us from the unhappiness and complications of sinful lifestyles.

Have you noticed how advice columnists are typically asked questions that relate to the difficulties resulting from sin? Here is one sad, typical column:

> Dear Ann Landers:
>
> I'd like to share my story because I know a lot of people think of their lives the way I thought of mine.
>
> Sometimes you feel lonely and unloved in a marriage—even after 23 years. You feel as if there's got to be more to life, so you set out to find someone who can make you blissfully happy. You believe you have found that someone and decide he is exactly what you want. So you pack up and say good-bye to your 23-year marriage and all the friends you made when you were part of a couple. You give your children the option of coming with you or staying with their father.
>
> You live the glorious life for a few years, and then a light bulb goes on in your empty head. You realize that you have exactly the life you had before—the only difference is that you've lost your friends, your children's respect and the best friend you loved and shared everything with for 23 years. And you miss him.
>
> You realize that love doesn't just happen, it must be nurtured through the years. You cannot undo what has been done, so you settle for a lonely and loveless life with emptiness in your heart.[2]

The complications in people's lives because of sin are incredible. Dysfunctional families litter the landscape of our nation; immoral lifestyles abound; those past the age of child rearing are forced to raise their children's children. I'm sure we have no idea how much money is spent because of sin, from home and airport security systems to higher prices because of shoplifting, to the need for prisons, border guards, and loan bailouts.

One of the first scriptures I remember memorizing was Psalm 119:9,11, which says, "How can a young man keep his way pure? By living according to your word. . . . I have hidden your word in my heart that I might not sin against you." It is possible to stay pure! Staying pure in body would mean no sexually transmitted diseases would be spread and no children would be born to unwed couples. Keeping pure mentally would mean wiping out pornography. Staying pure emotionally would mean demonstrating proper attitudes. Remaining pure spiritually would mean living our lives in service to God and others.

God Rewards Obedience

The results of a pure life should be all the motivation we need to obey God. But God, knowing us as He does, gives us other good reasons to obey. He says, "You know what else I'll do for you if you obey Me? I'll reward you!" God's Word will not only make us wise and give us life, joy, and direction, but God says that in keeping His commandments there is great reward (Psalm 19:11).

What rewards? I'd say "let me count the ways," but God's rewards are so many that would be an impossible task. A fascinating study for you would be to look up *reward* in a concordance and begin a list. Then, as you read the Bible each day, keep adding to your list. But for the moment, let's knock on the reward door and just peek in.

God rewards obedience by giving us a prolonged life (Proverbs

3:2), favor and a good name (3:4), and joy (10:28). He also promises knowledge (Proverbs 1:7) and wisdom (2:10), things I've longed for all my life! I think of knowledge as knowing facts and wisdom as the ability to apply those facts to life.

When God began to nudge me to write a book about the tongue, I held up my hands in horror and said, "No way! I can't do that, Lord, because I have too much trouble with my own speech." But God kept urging me to write it anyway. So with fear and trembling, some friends and I began to study what the Word says about the tongue. As we studied, God gave us knowledge of some of the good and evil aspects of the words we speak. Then as we prayed, God began to give us wisdom as to how we should apply those truths to our lives. The rewards were immediate! I became aware of many personal habits of speech that were hurtful and unkind, and God helped me begin to work on them. As I gained some knowledge and wisdom, God continued to give me more. He began to reward me with two more qualities that result from obedience: discretion and understanding (Proverbs 2:11). I became more aware of when to speak and when not to speak (discretion), and as I learned to listen, I grew in understanding.

The success of our Christian life is based on obedience. It is impossible to become godly women if we don't obey God.

To Love Is to Obey

There's a house in Colorado Springs that I glance at almost every time I drive by it. It sits high on a cliff opposite Palmer Park, and I call it "The Stilt House" because the whole front of the house is supported by visible braces, or "stilts," on the face of the cliff. I've never given a thought to that house falling off the mountain because it's obvious that those braces are pounded into solid rock.

The house invariably reminds me of Christ's admonition to build our life's foundations on rock rather than on shifting sands that collapse when the rains come and the winds blow. He spoke these clear words of warning: "Therefore everyone who hears these words of mine and *puts them into practice* is like a wise man who built his house on the rock" (Matthew 7:24, emphasis mine).

"Puts them into practice . . ." Christ was speaking of obedience here, and He emphasized that when He said, "If you love me, you will obey what I command" (John 14:15). It's as simple—and difficult— as that.

If you're struggling with this, I understand. I have agonized over it many times. It's much easier for me to think, *Oh, God loves me, and He'll understand my laziness or halfhearted willingness or skipping this altogether.* Studying God's desire for my obedience makes me more than uncomfortable; it makes me squirm! However, if I am serious about becoming the woman God wants me to be, I have to be convinced and convicted that disobedience isn't an option. Receiving the promises and blessings of God depends on my obedience to His Word.

I used to struggle with the concept of abiding in Christ talked about in John 15 (NASB). The results of abiding are tremendous: fruit of life, answered prayer, joy. But what does it really mean to "abide"? I had a hard time grasping that concept until someone asked me, "How do you spell *abide* with four letters?" I looked blank until he said, "O-B-E-Y."

Exactly. To love God is to obey Him. To obey God is to love Him. To abide is to obey, and to obey is to abide.

KEYS TO A GODLY LIFE

If you're ready to get serious about God and obeying His every word, there are several things you'll want to do regularly. The first is to ask God to show you through His Word what He wants you to focus on in your commitment to obedience.

Search Scripture

Before you read Scripture during your daily devotional time, take a moment to pray that God will impress on your heart His words for today. Many times He will highlight a promise for you to savor; other times He will bring to your attention a command for you to begin working on. Write down what God reveals. Think about the promise and thank God for it. Give attention to the command, and ask for His wisdom to apply it and obey it. He may lead you to write out a personal application for this verse and give you specific directions for obeying it.

When you hear a Bible-based sermon, take notes and pray about the message, asking God if He has said something through the speaker on which you should act.

Seek Counsel

Have you ever asked your best friend, husband, or children, "What do you see in my life that I should be working on?" I know, that's a tough one. It takes courage and humility and a great desire to grow—because they may tell you! And their words may hurt. But the people closest to you can be the best source of helping you see areas of your life that need to be conformed to the image of Christ.

Last year a friend was faithful enough to say to me, "Carole, do you realize that you are critical about many church worship services and speakers—and you don't have much good to say about the government either?" I winced inwardly. But as I thought about it, I realized she was right: I needed to obey God when He tells me to "Be kind and compassionate" (Ephesians 4:32).

Heed Criticism

How I hate to be criticized! No matter how kindly someone tells me something I've done wrong, I feel devastated. I tend not only to take it personally (don't we all?) but magnify it until I wonder, *If I'm like that or did that, how can anyone in the world like me?* I'm getting slightly better about this, but not much! However, I am learning to take to the Father any criticism I receive, lay it out before Him, ask Him to help me discern what's true and right and throw out what's not, be grateful to the person who brought it to my attention, and then do something about it.

Recently I received a critical letter from a person I didn't know. She felt my comments on forgiveness in my book *Marriage Takes More Than Love* weren't complete and could be misunderstood. I examined that chapter and concluded she was right, and so, in the next edition, I rewrote the chapter. But it's a lot easier to change something we've written than something we've done or said, isn't it? When we've hurt someone, most of the time all we can do is say we're sorry and ask forgiveness. Once in a while we can make restitution. But unless our wrong behavior is brought to our attention, chances are we'll continue it. So let's listen to criticism, evaluate it before the Lord, and then follow His directions on whether to throw it out or act upon it.

Make Hard Choices

I saw in action one man's determination to obey God no matter what. Some gray showed around his ears, a few lines of wisdom parenthesized his mouth, but the enthusiasm of a youthful spirit brightened his eyes. As his story unfolded, the group around the table listened raptly.

After becoming a committed Christian, Bill started Bible studies with the collegians working at the restaurant and casino he managed in Nevada. When a number came to Christ, they stopped spending their pay in gambling. The owner took notice. One day he called Bill in and told him to stop the Bible studies or he would lose his job.

"So," Bill said, "I quit my job."

"You gave up your *job?*" one man asked, incredulous.

"Of course I quit my job," Bill responded with a level look. "Some men give their *lives* to obey God."

Whatever happened to obedience? Whatever happened to making hard choices? Bill has a pretty good idea!

Making Biblical Truth Yours

Once again, start with some *verse studies*, praying that God will cement to your heart the need to be obedient to His Word.

- What keeps us from sin: Psalm 119:9-11
- The connection of love and obedience: John 14:21
- The relationship between obedience and joy: John 15:10-11

Next, do a *chapter (section) study* on James 1:22-26. For instructions on how to do a chapter study, see chapter four, page 56.

Finally, read 1 Samuel 15 and 2 Samuel 12:13, and contrast Saul's and David's responses to God's admonition when they disobeyed. Why do you think God rejected Saul as king? What do you think of the term *partial obedience?* In what areas of life are you tempted to partially obey?

CHAPTER SEVEN

Loving Your Husband

Occasionally, even after many years of marriage, the bad dream returns. I dream I'm back in college trying to get Jack's attention in a variety of ways—fainting, getting angry, leaving—but Jack totally ignores me, leaving me feeling rejected, lonely, and desperate.

It never happened. In that awful senior college year when Jack and I broke our engagement three times, he never ignored me. Quite the opposite. We would break up, I'd take off for a consoling weekend with my family, and he'd follow me. But still, the dream reveals how I felt inside during part of that year.

Jack's and my biggest problem was that we had the erroneous idea that love was a *feeling*. When the pressures of studies and other activities got to a critical point, some of the fun and excitement in our relationship dissipated. When this happened, we thought love had slipped away. Looking back on that time, we realize that we never stopped loving each other, even though the feeling of being in love was stifled.

After two years of marriage, we'd learned a few things about love. One day during the high-pressure days of seminary and working full-time, we found ourselves not only getting on each other's nerves but wondering where the fun of being married had gone. This time, however, we got down on our knees together before the Father and prayed that He would restore the joy to our relationship. We also began to work harder on our attitudes as well as look for creative ways to spend time together. The joy began to flood back in.

From the media today, we learn all the wrong things about love. Most movies and books give us the impression that love is sex, lust, desire, and "moonlight and roses" and that people fall in and out of love as quickly as they change clothes. God teaches something else entirely.

LOVE IS A FEELING TO BE LEARNED

Of the seven things listed in Titus 2:3-5 about which younger women are to learn, the first one is to love their husbands. When the apostle Paul wrote his letter to Titus, most marriages were arranged by the parents of the bride and groom. Brides probably never thought about falling in love, because in many cases they didn't even *meet* their husbands until their wedding day. Marrying for love wasn't even an option. But they were to love their husbands, nonetheless.

We approach marriage quite differently today. We wait until we fall in love with someone before we think about marrying him, which usually means we have a physical and sexual attraction to him. In most cases, authentic lasting love hasn't been tested or developed yet. Most of us enter marriage with only a vague idea of what real love is, and most wives need help to know how to fulfill this biblical command to love their husbands. We need to *learn* to love.

There are at least five different kinds of love that need to be brought together within marriage: There is friendship love, romantic love, sexual love, the "I'm-secure-with-you" kind of love, and *agape* or Christlike selfless love. When Jack and I got married, we were friends but not best friends. We had sexual love and some romantic love but knew little of the "belonging" (I'm-secure-with-you-and-I-can-trust-my-life-to-you) love or the agape, Christlike love. And two-and-a-half out of five isn't very good! However, I've met women who lacked even the two-and-a-half, who have gotten married to escape an unpleasant family situation or who have mistaken sexual desire for love. I know others who have married for security or to avoid being alone.

Friend, you may have married for some reasons that aren't holding your marriage together very well. You may feel stuck in a relationship that was never meant to be. Or you may appreciate your husband but feel that there is probably some other man out there who would be better suited to you. When you took those marriage vows, however, you promised to love and cherish *until death do you part*. So what can you do now?

Do you realize that God never gives a command that He doesn't give you the ability to carry out? God doesn't say "love your husband" without giving you the capability, the means, and the ideas (through His Holy Spirit living within you) with which to do just that. (Want to shout "Hallelujah!" now?) As you get to know God through His Word, you tap into His infinite wisdom concerning all sorts of things—and how to love your husband is one of them.

APPRECIATING YOUR CALLING AS A WIFE

Before you can understand how to love your husband, you need to be convinced that being a wife is a calling from God. Most of us don't understand the significance of God's sovereignty: that He ordains each and every day in our lives, even before a single one comes to be (see Psalm 139:16). God has a design for your life, and whatever that design may be, it is His special and unique calling for you. He may call you to work with handicapped children, go to China, or be a computer operator . . . and He may call you to be a wife.

A recent telephone survey reminded me I still need help with this truth. I was hastily answering the caller's persistent questions when she asked, "And what do you do?" I hesitated, then said, "I'm a writer." After hanging up the phone, I thought about my answer. True, I often write. But being a writer is my avocation, not my vocation. I do lots of things—drive a car, cook, lead Bible studies, clean house, speak, counsel people. But my vocation is to be a wife. Jack's wife. It is my most important call from God—my primary ministry. One meaning of the Hebrew word for woman is "the counterpart of man, made to be his helpmeet."[1] I am Jack's counterpart, completing him and helping him be what God wants him to be. And this frees me to be all God wants me to be as well.

If you are a wife, then know you have been called by God to be a wife. Knowing and understanding this can help you in a couple of important ways. First, such an understanding will sustain you through difficulties. Would you like to erase some days? Most wives have days when they wonder why they ever got married—days when they feel miserable, lonely, unloved, discouraged, and frustrated. On those days, especially, it will help to remember you are not in this situation by chance. You are *called* by God, just as a missionary is called to the mission field.

A missionary friend wrote that when she was depressed, lonely, sick, or feeling her work was in vain, she would remind herself of why she was there. She hadn't gone on a whim or for adventure or excitement; she had gone because she'd been *called by God* to go, and she was obeying God by being there.

Once I realized this truth applied to marriage as well, I wasn't as overwhelmed when difficulties came. I knew God would use life's problems and hardships, including my marital difficulties, to perfect me, to help me know Him and be fruitful for Him. I remember one period in our marriage when Jack's job required him to travel over half the time. At first my heart rebelled. I thought, *I didn't marry this man to have him gone all the time—and leaving me without a car, too!* But as I prayed, God spoke: "Carole, who meets your needs?"

"Well, I thought Jack was supposed to meet them."

"Wrong!" God answered. "No human can ever meet all your needs." The verse flashed into my heart, "And my God will meet all your needs according to his glorious riches in Christ Jesus" (Philippians 4:19).

"Oh," I said. "You mean You'll meet my need for companionship, someone to listen and talk to? You'll protect me, care for me, be the 'lifter' of my head?"

"Yes," God answered.

And I learned He can do all that . . . and more. During that time He became, in a real way, my husband (see Isaiah 54:5). Of course, being me, I went overboard the other way. When Jack called to say he'd be a day later getting home than planned, I cheerily assured him, "Oh, that's fine. Don't worry about it." (I was greatly disappointed, but I knew God would take care of my needs.)

A couple of days after Jack returned, he confessed, "You know, I get the feeling I'm not needed around here anymore." *Oh, no!* I thought. *What have I done now?* So I went back to God and asked Him about it. And He cleared up my confusion.

It is *God* who meets every need in my life, yet He often chooses to do it through my husband, my daughter, or my friends. At the same time if my husband (or others) can't or won't meet my need, God can and will, so I don't have to be disgruntled, discouraged, or despondent. This truth has helped me many times throughout my life, and it's one that every woman—single and married—needs to learn . . . and relearn.

A second way that understanding your calling as a wife can help you is by enabling you to keep sight of your priorities. Last week a missionary phoned and tearfully told me about a year of painful problems with her children that stifled any time or energy for a ministry of her own. She lamented this lost year. But she also said that her husband was having a very fruitful ministry and was loving every minute of it.

As we talked, I reminded her of something she knew but had forgotten in that difficult year: Her year hadn't been fruitless. She had given her time and energy to the three top priorities in her life: loving God, loving her husband, and loving her children. When we remember that God has called us first to be a wife and mother, we can keep our other responsibilities and goals in alignment with our primary purpose.

HOW TO REALLY LOVE YOUR HUSBAND

How do I learn to love my husband in the way the Bible commands? That's the question of a lifetime.

God spells it out for us clearly. In the *Amplified Bible,* Ephesians 5:33 lists some of the qualities included in reverencing one's husband.

> And let the wife see that she respects and reverences her husband [that she notices him, regards him, honors him, prefers him, venerates, and esteems him; and that she defers to him, praises him, and loves and admires him exceedingly].

In 1 Peter 3:2, even that list is added to. It says:

> [You are to feel for him all that reverence includes: to respect, defer to, revere him—to honor, esteem, appreciate, prize, and, in the human sense to adore him, that is, to admire, praise, be devoted to, deeply love, and enjoy your husband].

That's all you have to do!

Did you just throw up your hands and say, "Impossible!" It *would* be impossible, too, except for God's help, who told us we can do *all things* through Christ, who gives us strength (Philippians 4:13). You and I will never live up to these things 100 percent until we're in heaven, but that doesn't mean we aren't to work on them right here on earth. How do we do that? What does loving our husbands the way God wants us to *look* like?

Respect Him

Mary was a young woman who wanted to be obedient to God and to be a good wife, but she struggled with how to honor her husband.

"But I don't respect him," she explained. Her eyes filled with dismay as she continued, "He's lazy, sits around and watches TV all evening, ignores the children and me, doesn't seem to care about his appearance. How can I respect a person like that?"

Jean, a godly older woman sat quietly for a moment and then answered, "This command isn't optional, Mary, so let's consider this seriously. First of all, you must remember that you don't respect your husband because he *deserves* it but because God *commands* it. You are doing it out of obedience to God, not for the sake of your husband. That, in itself, may make a difference—especially when you remember that God won't give you a command without giving you the ability to do what He says."

Jean could tell Mary wasn't convinced, but she continued. "May I suggest that every day at the top of your prayer list you ask for grace to respect your husband?" Mary nodded slowly. She could do that much.

"Next," Jean continued, "why don't you write down every single thing about your husband that you do respect about him. What made you fall in love with him, for instance? Does he take care of the lawn? The car? Does he work to help support you and your children? Is he kind to the children? Does he have a sense of humor? Does he give to the church? Does he have friends? If so, what do they like about him? When you finish the list, try reading it over every morning. When negative thoughts come, read it again. Pick one thing each week to praise your husband about specifically and sincerely. Will you do that?"

"Yes," Mary responded. "I'll try."

That was the beginning of a whole new phase in Mary's relationship with her husband. When she praised him for what she did respect about him, he began to try harder in other areas of their relationship.

Praise can do that, you know. I think it was Elisabeth Elliot who said that when you get married you may like 80 percent of what your husband is and does and dislike 20 percent. The happiness of your marriage will depend on which percent you concentrate on. How true!

Dr. Ed Wheat wrote:

> God has designed marriage so that a husband is dependent on the affirmations of his wife, the appreciation she shows him for all that he gives her, and her demonstration of respect for his manhood. It is wounding when a husband criticizes his wife. It is equally wounding when the wife criticizes what her husband provides for her.[2]

Have you ever wondered about the meaning of the words, "An excellent wife is the crown of her husband" (Proverbs 12:4, NASB)? As I've puzzled over these words, I've concluded that they have a lot to do with respect and reverence. A crown sets the wearer apart as being someone very special. In other words, an excellent wife makes her husband feel special, and one of the ways she does this is by letting him know in many different ways that she respects him. Try it! Make it a practice to say often, "Honey, I respect you for . . ." or "I respect your ability to . . ." (About Jack I'd say, "balance the checkbook," "be the leader God meant you to be," "hit a golf ball," "plan a trip," "help me get on top of my schedule," "make good decisions.") And those are just a few of the things I've learned to respect about Jack.

Respecting your husband also means consciously choosing *not* to do certain things. How many times have your remarks about your husband cast him in a negative light—remarks such as "Jim was in a horrible mood this morning"; "he's a stickler for our budget until *he* decides to buy something"; "he never remembers my birthday"? Rather than setting him apart with respect and honor, those kinds of words portray your husband as an individual with glaring faults.

Recently I was reminded of the negative impact such words have. A friend and I were enjoying a beautiful evening on a lakeshore. The moon's reflection shimmered on the water around the dock. When I commented on the beauty of the moment, she responded, "Yes." After a small pause, she added, "But my husband would never notice." Into my mind popped the image of a grim-faced, unromantic clod—and I hadn't even met her husband.

According to Dr. Willard Harley in his book *His Needs, Her Needs,* one of five primary male needs is admiration.[3] Men need to know that their wives think of them as unique and remarkable.

If you're having trouble respecting your husband, try affirming him both in your private communication and in how you represent him to other people. You might be amazed at how your feelings for him change.

Adore Him

We're to *what?* Adore? Isn't respecting him enough? No, we are to genuinely admire our mate, praise him, and be devoted to him. While adoration is a feeling that can't be manufactured, adoring is demonstrated by actions. So let's reverse the order. Could it be possible that when we act adoring, our behavior will produce the feeling? I think so. But even if it doesn't, our actions—done as unto the Lord—will please God and greatly enhance our marriage relationship.

Generally you can easily spot a newly engaged or married couple. Last week Jack and I attended a Bible conference and sat four rows behind a couple I couldn't help noticing. They appeared to be in their late sixties. He kept his arm around her protectively while they sang from the hymnal, when they stood as the speaker prayed, when they sat down to listen to the sermon. Frequently she looked up at him and smiled, and he often leaned toward her to touch her cheek or whisper something in her ear. Theirs was the language of lovers everywhere. That afternoon when we visited a friend's motor home, the RV of the couple I'd observed was parked nearby. I wasn't surprised when our friend told me that the man, widowed for a year, had gotten married just two months before.

Adoring is demonstrated by glances, touches, and tone of voice, but it is also shown by complimenting, listening intently, asking his opinion, doing extraspecial things, telling him in a hundred ways how important he is to you. And it's possible to sustain such adoration throughout a marriage.

Part of adoring your husband is preferring to be with him. Prefer means "to put before something or someone else in one's liking, opinion, etc.; to like better." At a marriage seminar Jack and I were teaching, I began to notice the constant coming and going of many women in the group. Upon inquiry I discovered they were leaving to chauffeur children for everything from soccer games to birthday parties. Mothers need to do that sometimes, but this was supposed to be a special weekend for couples *together*. Often the wives were not present to do the couple assignments or to hear what might improve their marriages. As I talked with a number of husbands that weekend, they told me that, in their opinion, the children were their wives' number-one priority, routinely placed before the husbands' needs.

Quiz time: With whom do you prefer to go out to lunch? Go to a movie? Play a sport? Spend a day in the mountains? Pray? Discuss an important topic? Who takes your husband to the airport when he leaves on a business trip? Would you interrupt your child's nap to pick up your husband from work? When he asks, "Do you want to run errands with me?" do you excuse yourself because you've got better things to do? When he watches a sports event, do you ever sit with him just because you want to be with him? When was the last time you consciously paid your husband a compliment or did some special thing just to show how important he is to you?

I'm sure you didn't answer yes to every question, but honestly, do you prefer to be with your husband *most* of the time?

In order to prefer someone's company, you have to be friends. Best friends. If you feel that you and your husband are not best friends, I recommend that you read books on friendship, on marriage, on communication, on temperaments. Friendship is *developed*. You have to work on it, take time for it, pray about it, and give it priority.

Enjoy Him

In her book *Creative Counterpart*, Linda Dillow wrote:

> I have a dear friend whose husband is an avid fisherman. When they were newly married, he suggested they go fishing. Because she had heard that the family that plays together, stays together, she went. She recounted that the first time she put a minnow on a fishing hook, she was sure she would vomit. As with most things, it got easier, until soon she could do it without closing her eyes!
>
> Now, many years and four children later, she is thankful she became interested in her husband's interests. She recently said, "Linda, do you know the best time

> Bruce and I had last year? It was at 6:00 A.M. cleaning fish
> by the lake. The children were asleep, and we talked of
> deep and wonderful things we rarely talk about, as we
> cleaned the fish. I thanked God that morning that I had
> been willing to put that first minnow on the hook."[4]

To show genuine interest in our husband's interests is more important than most of us realize. Often, in the flush of first love, we feign an interest (or perhaps we really are interested because we love the man and whatever interests him interests us). But after we're married, we decide we really don't like football, or wrestling, or fishing—and so we urge our husband to do his favorite activities with friends and secretly hope he will give them up altogether.

I firmly believe that when God commands wives to "adapt yourselves to your husbands" (Ephesians 5:22, PH), he puts in women the innate ability to do just that. But many of us don't even try, much less pray that God will help us enjoy what our husbands enjoy. When we ask God to help us, *anything* is possible. I think of a petite singer who told me that before she married she got dizzy climbing a ladder. Wouldn't you know she married a man who loved mountain climbing? I looked at her with consternation and asked, "What did you do?"

"With prayer and determination," she answered, "I now climb mountains with him!"

It took me a long time to learn this one, but both Jack and I have worked on enjoying what the other enjoys. For instance, ten or so years ago I made a deliberate choice to pray about learning—and liking—to play golf. For years I had many excuses *not* to play (I'm one of the world's worst athletes, in almost any sport), but then Jack injured his knee and had to stop playing tennis and some other sports I enjoyed. I began to pray for two things: enough ability so I wouldn't be intimidated to death on the golf course, and the capacity to enjoy the game.

I took a few lessons and began. At first my enjoyment was just in the beauty of the outdoors and in being with Jack, but now, even though I'm still *really* bad, I do enjoy playing the game. And doing this together has been frosting on the cake of our happiness.

But there's another ingredient to enjoyment. Some husbands and wives don't enjoy each other because of an irritating habit—some glaring fault in a spouse's behavior that prevents true enjoyment of the other's company. I've heard comments such as:

"I don't enjoy going out to eat because my husband's manners are so crude."

"My wife is so disconnected in her speech I can't converse with her."

"In all our years together, my wife has never complimented me."

"I feel like he's mad at me much of the time."

"She's let herself go and doesn't even try to be attractive."

"I can't get him to talk about anything except football."

As you read this list, did you identify or add some of your own? If so, what can you do about it? God's Word sheds light on this dilemma. Proverbs 27:17 (NASB) says, "Iron sharpens iron, so one man sharpens another." One of the purposes of marriage is to sharpen each other so that we become more like Jesus and reflect the glory of God in our lives. To do that, we have to learn to address the negatives. Granted, dealing with negatives requires maturity on the part of both spouses. It requires that both people work at the relationship and be willing to change.

You may be thinking, *But my husband isn't willing to listen or to change*. In this case there is only one thing you can do: Pray for him. I mean *really* pray for him. Put all those things you'd like to confront him with on a prayer list, and pray for him every day. Most of all, pray that you will love and accept him and that God will give you the ability to adjust to him and to overlook (and even love) the very things that are irritating you now. Then pray that he will be open to talk about some of the other things. Most of all, pray that you will be willing to change behavior that is irritating to *him*, even if he is unwilling to change behavior that is unattractive to you. (I'm not talking about abusive behavior here—which should not be tolerated but must be worked through with a godly counselor—but rather irritating and unattractive habits.)

You can't change your husband. Only God can. Conversely, he can't change you. But God can, and He can make you willing to listen to your husband and be open to him. God can help you adjust in ways that will make you more enjoyable to be with. When you become more fun to be with, your husband might agree to change for you, too.

I hope that you, as a wife, put at least two things on your daily prayer list concerning your marriage: that God will deepen your love for your husband every day, and help you to understand him more and more. Someone has said, "To understand is to love." There's truth to that. As I've studied Jack—his strengths and weaknesses, his personality and character, his spiritual gifts, his likes and dislikes, what makes him laugh or makes him angry—I've not only grown to love him more, but I enjoy him more as well. We've both used a number of temperament analysis tools and been helped by them. I've read dozens of books on marriage and communication and grown in communication skills. I've learned also to appreciate our differences—which are many.

I'd like to encourage you to do two more things: (1) Ask your creative God for ideas on how to enjoy the man He gave you for a husband. God made him, and God will give you wisdom concerning him. You can count on it. (2) Begin to look around for someone who has been married awhile and who obviously loves her husband, and latch on to her. Pray that God will lay it on her heart to help you. Then ask her to meet with you, and have your list of questions ready. Often we come to a deeper understanding of God and His Word from another person who has gone ahead of us.

A LIFELONG ASSIGNMENT

In this chapter we've only skimmed the surface of what it means to love our husbands. I find I'm still learning what it means to love Jack. Charlie Shedd wrote, "True love has no maximum." And it's true. We will never exhaust the facets and depths of love. It will take you months to begin to probe the depths of Ephesians 5:31 and 1 Peter 3:12, but those are good places to start. If it seems impossible, please don't be discouraged. Instead, look on it as an adventure that you and God are going to do together—because that's exactly what it is.

As I write this, Jack and I are in the California desert, staying in a little one-bedroom condo. Jack has set up his computer on a table in the bedroom, and I'm hard at work with my computer on a card table in the living room. Several times this morning, just as I was concentrating on rewriting a paragraph, Jack called, "Hey, look what I've discovered!" (He's having a ball discovering shortcuts in a computer program.) My temptation is to say, "It'll have to wait. I'm in the middle of a thought." And he would understand. But the next time he wanted to show me something that was exciting to him, he'd hesitate about disturbing me. And I don't ever want him to hesitate. So I stop where I am and go in to find out what he's excited about. I haven't always done this. (I don't always do it now!) But I'm learning that this can be a way of demonstrating love, and it continues to bring us closer as a couple.

Two thousand years ago, Paul wrote that loving a husband is a priority for wives. Some things never change. This is one of them.

Making Biblical Truth Yours

Do the following *verse studies*:

- Ephesians 5:1
- 1 Corinthians 13:4-8
- 1 Peter 4:8

Next, do a *chapter study* on Proverbs 31:10-31. Outline the entire section and list the characteristics of the Proverbs 31 woman. Pick one for personal application.

As part of your study on loving your husband, try a bit of self-examination. Here are some questions to ask yourself. (Be honest—you and God are the only ones who will know your answers.)

- When was the last time your husband or someone else made a suggestion to you and you said (or thought), "But that's just the way I am"?

- How open are you to your husband's or others' suggestions for changes you need to make in your life?
- When was the last time God showed you something you should change? (If He doesn't do it frequently, you've stopped listening!)

Here are some other things you can do to grow in love for your husband:

- Make a prayer list for yourself of traits in your life and personality that have been criticized either by your husband, someone else, or God. Ask God to give you concrete ways to work on changing these things.
- Make a list of interests that you and your husband can share, and begin to pray for wisdom in choosing one to develop.
- Pray that you and your husband will have more fun together, and ask God for ideas on how you can do that.
- Pray that you will develop as friends and that you will increasingly enjoy one another.
- Begin a list of books to read to develop your love, and commit to reading at least one each month. You may want to begin with the book Jack and I wrote, *Marriage Takes More Than Love* (NavPress). I also recommend Dr. Ed Wheat's *Love-Life for Every Married Couple* and Norm Wright's *Communication, Key to Your Marriage*. Ask your friends for books that have helped them in their marriages.

CHAPTER EIGHT

Loving Your Children

My niece was awakened in the middle of the night when Melissa, her seven-year-old daughter, padded into the bedroom.

"Are you having a bad dream, honey?" Melody asked sleepily.

"No. I just feel funny."

"Are you sick?"

"No, Mommy. I just have this funny feeling."

"Well, why don't you crawl into bed with me for a few minutes?"

Melody put her arms around her small daughter and asked, "What will help this feeling?"

Melissa answered by snuggling close. Then she said with a contented sigh, "You." After a few minutes she went back to her own bed feeling safe and secure.

Melody has learned how to love her children. She had a great role model in her own mother, my sister Joye, and she's also learned from the examples of others. But mostly, I think, she's learned it from God.

Paul, inspired by God, told Titus that one of the things women must learn is to love their children. Fewer and fewer girls today are growing up with godly role models. Some have never seen love in a family, either between parents or between parents and children. Or if they had loving parents, sometimes those parents weren't Christians, so the children-turned-parents have no training in how to help their own children mature in Christ. And yet, since God commands Christian mothers to love their children, that must mean it's possible for them to learn how.

HOW TO REALLY LOVE YOUR CHILDREN

Love comes in more flavors than Baskin-Robbins ice cream.

Sometimes love must be tough—like taking a stand against unacceptable behavior.

Sometimes love is firm—like doing something different from what "everyone else's parents" are doing. When Lynn was fifteen, she had an 11:00 P.M. curfew, earlier than any of her friends (at least according to her). One Saturday night she called at midnight to say she and her date had left the party a bit late and then had a flat tire. I sat up (Jack was out of town) and waited for the two of them to appear. When they finally came in at 1:30 A.M., I explained firmly to Lynn's date that he was responsible for leaving a party early enough to get Lynn home on time. When he left, grim faced and sober, Lynn wailed, "MOTHER! He'll never ask me out again!" But he did . . . and he got her home on time from then on.

Sometimes love is tender—like crying with your children when they hurt and taking seriously what they take seriously. I remember how awful Lynn felt in the fifth grade when her first "crush" ignored her. She told me later how much she appreciated the fact that I didn't say, "Oh, honey, you'll get over it—it's just 'puppy love.'" Fortunately

I remembered how much "just puppy love" hurts, so I empathized and identified with her.

Sometimes love is fun. One time when Melody and her kids were having ice cream cones at home, Melody told the kids to close their eyes and open their mouths, and when they did, she sprayed their mouths full of whipped cream. They all had a good laugh together!

I asked three women I think are great moms—Melody, Sonja, and Lynn—to list ways they demonstrate love to their children. (They have eight children among them, ages seven to twenty-two.) Their replies were wise and varied:

- "I comfort them when they're afraid. I try not to discount the reason they're afraid unless it's to point out that while they aren't silly, what they're afraid of might be."
- "I apologize when I'm wrong."
- "I love their father."
- "I spend time with them, doing things they want to do. They have to do a lot of things with me that they don't want to do, but then we'll go to the park, the library, to their friends' houses, etc."
- "I give positive reinforcement on what they're doing well. These are specific and genuine compliments, not just flattery."
- "I resolved not to get angry with my children over inconsequential things like spilling milk, no matter how often or how big a spill it was. I'd just wipe it up and continue talking with them." (Now *that* takes self-control!)
- "My husband and I get involved with what our kids are interested in. We've learned a lot about soccer and go to all the games. We've also made an effort to get to know their friends, have

them over, host some parties. We have a rule at our house that once you've been here three times, you're considered family—with all its privileges and responsibilities. Consequently, I have two sets of quadruplets: one for our son, one for our daughter."

- "We tell them we love them and show them physically. Simple, but effective."

- "I let the children help with all sorts of things—a practice that makes the tasks take longer and often produces less-than-ideal results. But it shows them I want their help and value our time together."

- "I try to be patient! Impatience and inappropriate expectations of little ones don't show love."

- "I try to help them discover their strengths and encourage them to excel in a couple of things, be it chess, music, sports, or the arts."

- "We honor them as real people by not being condescending and by treating them with respect. Small example: We always knock on their bedroom doors and wait for an answer before going in. We thank them when they do us a favor, and we expect the same courtesy from them."

Friend, please take a minute here to think of ways you love your own children. You might want to make two lists—one of ways you demonstrate love now and another of ways you want to learn to love in the future.

Give Your Children LOTS of Time

Almost nothing demonstrates love like freely giving one of our most precious resources: time. The best thing you can do for your children is be willing and ready to *be there* when they want or need you.

While watching a Taco Bell commercial at 10:30 one night, Jana's thirteen-year-old daughter said she was hungry. "Let's go!" Jana said. And the two of them roared down to Taco Bell for a snack. The rest of the family wanted in on the fun, but this time was just for the two of them. Jana calls such opportunities "open windows," and she takes advantage of them even when she's tired or busy, because she realizes she won't always have them.

Late at night Kathy's fifteen-year-old son occasionally still calls, "Come tuck me in, Mom!" She laughs and says, "How can I tuck someone in who doesn't even fit on the bed anymore?" (Her son is 6'4".) But she knows that what he means is, "Come talk to me, Mom." And so they talk and talk about all kinds of stuff.

If you have more than one child, make sure that each one gets individual time and attention. I know that's hard, but it's important. I had a brother and sister, so personal times with my parents were rare. But I still remember the time Mom took just *me* for a hike and a picnic down by the dam. (I fell in and got my pants wet, and we dried them on a rock.) And I remember Dad taking just *me* with him on a couple of 4-H Club tours. Those were standout days for me because I had a parent all to myself.

My daughter Lynn took her son Eric out to lunch on his first Christmas vacation after he'd started college. I told her it was fun to see her have a date with him. She grinned and said, "I learned that from you." I reflected, then, on the visits we made to Mexico when Lynn's family lived there. On each visit I made a point to take Lynn out for lunch, my son-in-law, Tim, out for breakfast, Eric on a hike through the hills of the city, and Sunny to the market. I found that by ourselves we talked about entirely different things than we did as a whole family.

Here are some concrete ways to give your children quality time:

- Read to them and read with them, and as they get older, let them read to you.
- Take time to tell them stories—all kinds of stories—about when you were little, about when they were born, and what they did as a baby. Make up stories. (Even if you aren't good at it, they'll love it!) One of the girls who lived with us when Lynn was three started making up "George, the Friendly Wolf" stories, and when she moved, I carried them on. My grandchildren even became fans of George!
- Play games with them. Shoot hoops, play catch, get the whole family involved in a touch football game. Play all the board games your kids love. Yeah, I know "Candyland" is boring—but your children are not.
- Attend every concert, play, recital, speech presentation, sports event, and academic program that your children are in. If you want them to feel loved by you, your presence and support are crucial.

BE LOVING AND CONSISTENT IN YOUR DISCIPLINE

Many good books have been written about how to discipline a child, but I think there are just a few essential rules.

When You Say No, Mean It

In the small town where I grew up it was obvious that one mother of three "all boy" sons had done a terrific job with them. Strong, adventurous, rambunctious boys, they were nevertheless courteous and obedient. When asked her secret, she said, "I don't say no unless I have to, but when I say no, I mean it."

I thought of that as I sat talking with a young mother. Her small daughter was playing noisily in the room, and the scene went something like this:

Mother: Please go downstairs. We're trying to talk. (She might as well have been talking to the wall. The child went right on playing noisily.)

Mother: I said, go downstairs and play. (The child didn't budge.)

Mother (very firmly): Did you hear what I said? Go play downstairs!

Child: But I want to play up here.

Mother: You're bothering us. Play downstairs.

The child finally went halfway down the stairs, paused for a moment, then came back up and started playing again. The mother shrugged and smiled apologetically, and we continued our conversation. Actually, the child wasn't that distracting. But since her mom had given her a command, Mom should have followed through.

Parents need to decide together what the bottom lines are in their home at each stage of their children's lives. One of our guidelines for Lynn when she was three was that she couldn't cross the street alone. We lived in a cul-de-sac, and she was allowed to roam all over the cul-de-sac, but she was forbidden to cross to the other side of the street.

When Lynn was fourteen, the rules were different, of course. She could cross the street alone, but we were to be informed of her whereabouts, and she had a definite curfew. However, we tried to limit unnecessary rules so as not to frustrate her. (We probably did anyhow!)

Colossians 3:21 tells fathers, "Do not embitter your children, or they will become discouraged." I'm convinced that both having no rules and having too many rules contribute to embittering or, as another translation says, "provoking" children and discouraging them as a result. One of my own guidelines was, if I couldn't explain the rule so Lynn would understand it (not necessarily agree with it), I would reevaluate the guideline itself.

Discipline for Disobedience Only

If mothers could hear themselves after a day with their children, many would be shocked at how many times they tell their kids, "Don't do that!" They'd be horrified at the scolding, disapproving looks, and even whacks on the seats they give their children for things they never forbade the kids to do in the first place. For example, a child tracks in mud on the clean floor, and his mother scolds. But she never told the child, "Please wipe your feet before you come in. I've just mopped the floor." If she'd said that, and the child didn't wipe his feet, that would be disobedience and would call for appropriate discipline.

But a mother can't foresee everything a child thinks up, can she? When Lynn was in grade school, she decided to surprise me and make candles by melting a lot of old candles together in a pan. When the result looked too thick, she added water to the wax and then was horrified at the mess in the pan. She decided to get rid of the whole concoction by pouring it down the garbage disposal. When I walked in and saw the sink full of water and bits of wax, I nearly lost it. But I'd never told Lynn not to make candles, add water, and then pour the mess down the sink. It was a situation that called for patience on my part but not discipline, because she really didn't know any better and hadn't disobeyed me.

The next time you're provoked and feel like scolding, ask yourself, *Did this child disobey me or only inconvenience me?* Discipline for disobedience. Be patient with an inconvenience—even a major one like a stopped-up garbage disposal!

Give Appropriate Discipline in Love

Knowing the unique nature of each of your children is imperative here. Some children are crushed with a look. Others need a two-by-four to get their attention. (I'm not speaking literally here!) I remember visiting one couple who had five small children. While I was talking with the parents, one little girl who was sitting on the potty chair was happily drawing on the wall with a crayon. When her father finally noticed what she was doing, he interrupted our talk, walked over to her, and said, "Oh, Brenda, we've told you not to draw on the walls." Then he picked her up, took a small wooden paddle, and carried her to the basement. I could hear her wails. Then he carried her upstairs and held her close until her crying ceased, all the while crooning, "Brenda, Daddy loves you very much, but you must not disobey." When her sobs subsided, father and daughter had a good hugging session, and all was well. I've never seen any family get along as beautifully as that one. Today all five children are strong adults, serving the Lord.

Melody told me that when her son was caught lying and a warning didn't seem to work, she and her husband decided to make the punishment fit the crime. They didn't believe him about *anything* for a whole day. When they caught him lying again, they didn't believe him for two whole days. The lesson brought him to tears of frustration because he wanted to be believed, but they told him that trust had to be earned and he had broken that trust, so why should they believe anything he said? After that, they never had to repeat the lesson!

MODEL YOUR CONVICTIONS

Example really is the best teacher. You'll never teach your child honesty if you instruct her to tell a caller you aren't home when you are. You'll never help your kids to reject the junk and garbage the media offers if you're watching it yourself.

I can still see my father's face when I'd been given more change than I had coming at the grocery store. I thought it was a great deal, but Dad said, "Carole, whether you steal five cents or a million dollars, it's all the same. Stealing either one makes a person a thief." His statement has stayed with me throughout my life. Even when a vending machine started spewing pop and candy bars at a motel and our family thought we'd hit the jackpot, my father's voice was clear in my heart. So, our arms loaded with the bonanza, we reported to the reception desk. They looked incredulous and then said, "Keep it!" (An extra bonus for our honesty, I guess!)

"Don't let the world around you squeeze you into its own mold," warns Paul in Romans 12:2 (PH). As the world pushes harder against our moral values, it's easy to give inch by inch until, without even realizing it, we look, act, and think like the world. But God's command is clear: *Do not be conformed* (Romans 12:2, RSV).

LEARN HOW TO PARENT FROM GOD HIMSELF

Jack and I often say that the best marriage manual of all time is the Bible. And the best book on raising children is the Bible as well. Conflicting advice that comes from many so-called experts just leaves parents confused. But there is One who made children in the first place and knows all about them. The truths in Scripture are for all parents in any culture. The admonitions, warnings, commands, and guidelines transcend time and place, and we can—and should—stake our lives on them.

Zero in on Proverbs

I encourage you to begin honing your parenting skills by studying the book of Proverbs. Proverbs is full of topics concerning character traits and relationships, and you could spend months digging into these for wisdom about parenting. Wisdom means having the power to judge rightly and follow the soundest course of action, based on knowledge, experience, and understanding. Isn't that exactly what we parents need?

Start by reading through the entire book of Proverbs, a chapter a day. (This will take you one month.) Keep a page in a notebook with seven or eight topics that you feel are most critical for you to know. As you read a chapter, jot down the verses that speak to each subject. After finishing the list of verses, write a paragraph of observations and conclusions, as well as personal applications and steps to take to become a better parent and influence your children effectively.

Here is a partial list of subjects to consider studying:

- God's discipline (includes the connection between love and discipline): Proverbs 1:2-6; 3:11-12
- parents' discipline (why and how): Proverbs 13:24
- lying: Proverbs 12:19
- the tongue (what we say and how we say it, when to be silent, when to speak): Proverbs 10:11,18,19,21; 11:13; 12:15,25; 13:3; 18:2
- listening: Proverbs 18:13
- purity: Proverbs 21:21
- avoiding evil: Proverbs 16:6
- godly character traits: Proverbs 16:32; 17:9,27-28
- wisdom and discernment: Proverbs 1:7; 2:1-6,10-12
- trust in God: Proverbs 3:5-6
- guarding the heart: Proverbs 4:23
- the importance of knowing God's Word: Proverbs 7:1-3
- the importance of instruction (from God, parents, others): Proverbs 9:9; 10:8; 12:15; 15:31
- pride and humility: Proverbs 3:7; 11:2; 13:10; 15:33; 16:18; 28:13)
- what makes a peaceful home: Proverbs 15:17; 24:3-4
- the value of work: Proverbs 24:32-34
- getting counsel: Proverbs 15:22
- choosing friends: Proverbs 13:20; 17:9,17; 22:24
- giving: Proverbs 11:25
- what to look for in a spouse: Proverbs 12:4; 14:1; 31:10-31.

Let's explore how to study Proverbs by focusing on the subject of handling anger and losing your temper—something most parents and children can use help with. The page in your study notebook might look like this:

Handling Anger Appropriately

Verses:

Proverbs 13:3: "He who guards his lips guards his life, but he who speaks rashly will come to ruin."

Proverbs 13:10: "Pride only breeds quarrels, but wisdom is found in those who take advice."

Proverbs 15:1: "A gentle answer turns away wrath, but a harsh word stirs up anger."

Proverbs 16:18: "Pride goes before destruction, a haughty spirit before a fall."

Proverbs 16:32: "Better a patient man than a warrior, a man who controls his temper than one who takes a city."

Proverbs 17:27: "A man of knowledge uses words with restraint, and a man of understanding is even-tempered."

Proverbs 19:19: "A hot-tempered man must pay the penalty; if you rescue him, you will have to do it again."

Proverbs 22:24-25: "Do not make friends with a hot-tempered man, do not associate with one easily angered, or you may learn his ways and get yourself ensnared."

PROVERBS 29:11: "A fool gives full vent to his anger, but a wise man keeps himself under control."

PROVERBS 29:22: "An angry man stirs up dissension, and a hot-tempered one commits many sins."

Observations/Conclusions:

I am foolish when I lose control in anger.

I am wise when I stay in control of both my words and actions.

Personal Application:

God is using Proverbs 29:11 to speak to my heart. It says that a fool "lets it all hang out" but a wise person is in control. When I inadvertently pulled in front of a teenager's truck, he screamed and made obscene gestures and honked all the way down the street. Mentally I gave full vent to my anger and was steamed for about an hour. This week I'll memorize this verse and pray each day for control of my *spirit*.

As you study and write down verses from Proverbs on various topics, keep adding to them as you read through the Bible. Continue asking God to help you form deep convictions in your heart, then talk about them with your spouse, your minister, and other godly parents. As you do this, your own convictions concerning parenting will solidify.

Note to single women without children: If you don't have children of your own, you might consider "adopting" one or two—for your sake and theirs. Having children close is a wonderful way to learn patience, endurance, love, kindness, and unselfishness. You might want to volunteer to teach a child to read, to help in the church nursery, to baby-sit a friend's child for a morning twice a month. I hope you won't let yourself miss out on the joys—and the lessons—that come from being close to a child.

When Jack and I were rearing Lynn, we constantly asked God to give us wisdom. I can't think of anything more important when it comes to loving our children. Aren't you glad that God promised He'd give it to those who ask for it?

Making Biblical Truth Yours

Do the following *verse studies:*
- Proverbs 3:5-6
- Proverbs 22:6
- Deuteronomy 6:4-8

Next, using 1 Corinthians 13:4-13 as a guide, make a list of one thing you can do each day to put that kind of love into practice with your children. What quality do you need to develop most?

Finally, you may want to begin making a list of goals and desires for your children, keeping in mind that a goal is something you can control while a desire can only be prayed for. For instance, your desire may be to have a godly child, but you can't make that happen. Your goal needs to be something within your power to do, such as helping your child memorize one verse of Scripture each week or taking him or her to Sunday school.

CHAPTER NINE

Managing Your Household

I shuddered as the speaker said, "Your home reveals much about who you are." She went on to explain that she didn't mean how expensive your home was or how beautiful the furnishings were but rather what your home revealed about your sense of order, color, degree of neatness and cleanliness—things, she emphasized, that make a house a home.

One missionary husband observed, "Most women are nest makers. Women seem to have an innate need and desire to have a place. They can live a gypsy lifestyle only so long before becoming unduly stressed." Wise man.

Years ago when I was in college, I met a missionary wife who lived out in the jungle, hundreds of miles from civilization. She said all supplies had to be carried in on the backs of donkeys, yet she took three items with her wherever she went: a silver candlestick, a linen tablecloth, and a collage of pictures because, for her, these things made each hut a *home*.

Paul declared in Titus 2 that in addition to loving her husband and children, a woman is to be a "keeper at home" (v. 5, KJV). God has given us a need and desire to make a nest, have a place, and develop a house into a home. We may not hear a great deal about being a keeper at home these days, but God's Word isn't dated, and we need to examine and understand just what this means for us today.

BEING A KEEPER AT HOME

A lot of questions come to mind, I'm sure, and no doubt the first one is, Does being a keeper at home mean a wife isn't to work outside the home? Not necessarily. (You can breathe now!) When we read any scripture, we need to study other passages that relate to the subject to be sure we are understanding the real meaning of the verse. In this case, Proverbs 31:10-31 gives us some insight.

The Proverbs 31 woman is quite a lady. Pull back the curtain a moment and take a look at the flurry of her activity. First, she selects wool and flax and begins to work with it—not because she has to but because she wants to ("eagerly," it says in verse 13). Verse 14 says she goes out and gets food from a grocery store miles away (better bargains probably). If we watch her long enough, we observe her getting up before the sun in order to provide food, not only for her family, but for her servants, too (v. 15). (I wonder why she didn't ask the servants to do that.) As we watch her, we might say, "Well, all those tasks are ones the average housewife does, to a degree." But there's more! The woman in Proverbs 31 also has a couple of business ventures outside her home. She buys real estate and develops it into a profitable vineyard (vv. 16,18), and then to top it off, she starts a clothing store, making her own merchandise to sell (v. 24). Every time I read about this lady, I get tired. She worked both inside and outside the home— and had a great attitude doing it.

Maybe we can't all be like this model of industry, but working outside the home wasn't considered a no-no even back then. Being a keeper at home doesn't necessarily mean we can't work outside the home. However, I am convinced that a wife needs to evaluate her God-given priorities when trying to decide whether to work outside the home. Her priorities, according to the list in Titus 2, are . . .

God,

husband,

children,

and home.

Single women who are mothers obviously would focus on their children after God, but even for women who don't have a husband or children, being a "keeper at home" still ranks high according to Paul's teaching. While we are inclined to crowd into our lives other items such as career, education, and ministry, do you notice that in the Titus 2:3-5 list these are glaringly absent? When I realized this, I concluded that even my ministry or an outside job diminished in importance to being a keeper at home, and if that was the case, it was important for me to know what Paul really meant.

SHOULD YOU WORK OUTSIDE THE HOME?

May I (gently) suggest that when a wife and mother—one who is serious about obeying God—asks, "Should I work outside the home?" she is asking the wrong question. The first question a woman should ask is not, "Do we need the money?" Neither is it, "Can I pursue a career at the same time as being a homemaker?" nor, "Will it be fulfilling and something I want to do?" Often if the answer is yes to these questions, she plunges ahead. Instead, she should ask, *"Is this God's will for my life?"*

You may be thinking, *But doesn't God lead through circumstances?* Sometimes, but not always or primarily. God leads mainly through His Word (Psalm 119:105), through peace of heart (Philippians 4:6-7), and through the counsel of other people (Proverbs 15:22). If circumstances line up with the direction you get from these three primary channels, then they're an added bonus and may help you be assured of what God's will really is.

Let's assume that you really need the money from a job outside the home. So you and your husband pray about whether or not you should go to work. If God says no, He'll meet your need in other ways, miraculous ways sometimes. But if He says yes, He will give you the ideas, creativity, and strength to work outside the home and still maintain your God-given priorities.

What do you think of when you hear the phrase "keeper at home" or "keeping the home fires burning"? If you're anything like me, you picture a perfect little cottage with a white picket fence, tended garden, spotless kitchen, freshly baked bread, five kinds of cookies in an old-fashioned cookie jar, and you in a ruffled apron anticipating your children's arrival home from school. Frankly, I doubt that even first-century women lived up to that vision! So what does being a keeper at home really mean for you?

WHAT DOES THIS COMMAND MEAN FOR ME?

In our society where many wives work outside the home, biblical priorities, guidelines, and commands get fuzzy. If a husband and wife both provide family income, then it only seems fair that they share household responsibilities as well. Many working wives carry a deep resentment toward husbands who don't pick up and do their fair share of the work load around the house.

But wait. Where does this thinking come from? Do we have a scriptural basis for our view? Or are we buying into the world's system? Romans 12:2 says, "Don't let the world around you squeeze you into its own mold, but let God remold your minds from within" (PH). Are we getting squeezed? Scripture clearly delineates who is responsible for what in a marriage relationship. Biblical mandates cross cultures, generations, and economies, so it does no good to argue that times have changed, because God and His Word have not.

A husband is to:

- be the head of his home (Ephesians 5:23)
- provide for his household (1 Timothy 5:8)
- love his wife and care for her as his own body (Ephesians 5:28)

These are his responsibilities no matter what else he does.

A wife is to:

- respect her husband (Ephesians 5:33, 1 Peter 3:1)
- love her children (Titus 2:4)
- manage her household (1 Timothy 5:14)

How much a husband and wife help each other with their respective obligations is not the issue here; who is *responsible* for what is the issue. And Scripture declares women responsible for the home.

Let me clarify what I'm *not* saying. The majority of women today work two full-time jobs: one outside the home and one inside the home as wife, mom, and keeper of the home. Wives assume part of the responsibility of meeting financial obligations, and their husbands usually assume part of the responsibility within the home (and rightly so!). There's nothing unbiblical about husbands and wives sharing jobs and work loads; it's just that God gives specific *responsibilities* to each one.

A woman's God-ordained responsibility includes managing her household. In 1 Timothy 5:14 (RSV) Paul says that the younger widows are to "marry, bear children, rule their households," which to me helps explain being a keeper at home. Words for "rule their households" are translated "manage" (NIV), "guide the house" (KJV), "run their own households" (PH), and "preside over the house" (NEB).

The dictionary defines *manage* as "to have charge of; direct; conduct; administer." What does that mean today? To me, it simply means that I'm responsible to see that things at home run smoothly—that the machinery doesn't break down or grind to a stop and that the oil of love is liberally applied. It means keeping my house in reasonable order, seeing that food is on the table at mealtimes, keeping the household budget under control, and making sure my family stays as healthy as possible. And, I might add, doing this with a joyful attitude.

"All right, so the responsibility is mine!" you cry with your hands flailing in the air. "How can I possibly do everything that's on my plate?" Perhaps more simply than you think.

GETTING THE JOB DONE

Over the years I've learned some practical principles that have helped me begin to fulfill God's command that I manage our home and yet not be overwhelmed or exhausted. You may have heard this as the *K-I-S-S* principle which stands for "Keep It Simple, Stupid." But we'll eliminate that second *S*, okay? Here's the principle:

Keep the Management of Your Home Simple

Early in our marriage when Jack and I managed a servicemen's training home, stress and exhaustion accompanied my days. I had so much to do. After all, I wanted to be the best wife I could be. I thought I had to vacuum every day—because that's the way it had been done before. I thought I had to serve breakfast to all the men living with us early each morning—because that's the way it had been done before. I thought I needed to learn to cook some complicated, gourmet dishes—because I wanted to do it better than anyone had done it before. I found myself trying to live up to my own expectations, my husband's expectations, and my *perception* of everyone else's expectations as well. That's a hard thing to do!

I got some practical help from my mentor, Marion, and it saved my sanity. One of the things that took a hunk of time I didn't have was ironing the shirts of the four men who lived in our home, plus Jack's—and that was before polyester! It took me an average of two hours a day to do all those shirts. When I told Marion of my fatigue, she had me write down everything I was doing for one week. When I showed it to her, she said, "This is impossible. Let's trust God for the money to send out the shirts to be done professionally," which we did. I also began to make simpler meals and stopped vacuuming every day.

Never Assume You Know What Others Expect

Too often we put pressure on ourselves because of what we *think* someone else desires or expects. One woman I know says that when she first married, her husband—whose mother was a meticulous housekeeper—wasn't happy with the way she cleaned house, even though she tried her very best. Finally she had the wisdom to ask him, "What to you is a 'clean house'? If I have time to clean only one thing, what should it be?" To her great surprise he answered, "The bathroom medicine cabinet." He told her it was the first thing he saw when he got up in the morning, and to him it represented a "clean house." She discovered that when that cabinet was orderly, he was far less critical of the house in general.

I, too, learned the importance of asking about expectations. As a young wife I loved to try gourmet recipes, which took a great deal of shopping and cooking time I didn't have. I talked myself into thinking that I was doing it for Jack. But it wasn't long before I discovered that, while Jack liked some of what I cooked, he actually was a simple "meat and potatoes" kind of guy whose all-time favorite meal was (and is) a pot roast with mushroom soup on top, shoved in the oven and cooked to death. That's *his* idea of a gourmet meal and is one of the simplest meals I fix.

So *ask* about expectations. Ask your husband to name the top three things that make home comfortable to him. If one of those is neatness, follow up with, "What is a neat home to you?" (Everyone is different here. To me, if I don't make the bed first thing in the morning, the whole house looks like a disaster. But when I'm gone, Jack doesn't make the bed until I'm about to come home.) Ask him what three simple meals he enjoys most. What does he enjoy that is special when you have the time? Ask your children what their favorite foods are and what makes the home comfortable for them as well.

Don't Compare Your Homemaking Skills and Habits with Those of Others

We can learn a great deal from others if we'll observe, explore, and ask. When I saw a busy homemaker putting several layers of newspapers on the shelves that held her pans, I discovered it was a quick and efficient way to line the pan shelf (and cheaper than shelf paper, too). If we look at others in order to learn from them, we can benefit a great deal.

However, if you're like me, it's easy to look at others and compare yourself negatively rather than learn positive tips. I used to be intimidated by some of my mother-in-law's habits. At her home she had a different dishtowel for silverware, for dishes, and for pans. I had one dishtowel for everything except the worst pans, which I dried with a paper towel. She liked to have one napkin for her lap and one to wipe her hands on; I just had one. She wiped off every spot from the stovetop after every meal; I would give mine a lick and a promise every few days. It took me many years to accept the fact that although she did a number of things more beautifully than I could ever hope to do, Jack's mother accepted me—and loved me—just the way I am.

Even if you don't have an accepting mother-in-law, however, you can't live your life trying to meet other people's expectations. You'll go crazy trying. And remember, ultimately it is the Lord Christ we serve (Colossians 3:24), and He will always give us the ability to do what He asks us to do.

Remember That Guests Come to Visit You, Not to Evaluate Your Housekeeping Skills

First Timothy 5:10 describes one of the qualities a respected widow demonstrated: hospitality. Some of the things she did are spelled out:

She washed the feet of the saints, relieved the afflicted, and devoted herself to doing good in every way. A paraphrase for today's woman might read, "She reached out to everyone within her circle—friends, acquaintances, neighbors—helping them in any way possible. She especially was alert to people in need and opened her home and heart to them." Offering hospitality is one of our responsibilities as godly women.

I remember one woman telling me that when she arrived overseas to visit some friends, the couple was so exhausted the visit wasn't a happy one. As she was preparing to leave, she inadvertently discovered that to prepare for her visit they had literally scrubbed the house from top to bottom—including the walls! She was frustrated to learn that their desire to have things perfect for her had backfired by making them too tired to enjoy her company.

Romans 12:3 tells us to "try to have a sane estimate of your capabilities by the light of the faith that God has given to you all" (PH). In light of that verse, I think a woman needs to be wise about her own capabilities and gifts in every area, including homemaking and hospitality.

My sister, Joye, could laugh about the fact that she simply could not cook. She took a lot of good-natured kidding about her Jell-O not getting firm, her cakes falling, her meat being tough. But she was a whiz at making her guests feel comfortable, and she excelled in telling stories to her children and in teaching them kindness and love.

I used to feel guilty every time I read about how the woman in Proverbs 31 sewed clothes for her household. I expressed my concern to Jack, and he wisely told me that he would rather I bought our clothing and saved my time for what I enjoyed and could do well.

What a relief! Since then I've been able to keep a proper perspective on how God has gifted me in that area. (Well, actually, how He has *not* gifted me in that area!)

Being a keeper at home is a big task, but it won't be overwhelming if you keep trying to simplify your home (as well as your life) and striving to please God, not people. One saying I like is that while the husband is the hearth, the wife is the fire that warms the hearth. The man provides the leadership—he is the head; but the woman provides the warmth—she is the heart.

May God give you a heart to be His servant as you keep your home for Him.

Making Biblical Truth Yours

Before you even begin doing these Bible studies, would you write a paragraph on what managing a household means to you right now? How have your views been influenced by the world around you? How has your thinking changed through the years?

Now do some *verse studies* on the following:

- Romans 12:13
- 1 Timothy 5:10
- Hebrews 13:2
- 1 Peter 4:9-10

Look up Lydia (in Acts 16:13-15,40) and Phoebe (in Romans 16:1-2), and see what the Bible says about these women. How would you describe these women if you were telling your neighbor about them?

If you want a good book to read, I recommend Linda Dillow's *Creative Counterpart*. Write down pertinent points from it to discuss with a friend.

Finally, ask five godly older women to share their ideas about being a keeper at home. Take notes on what they teach you.

CHAPTER TEN

Getting a Grip on Self-Control

Jcan still remember it even though it happened years ago. Jack and I lived in the Chicago area and had taken a rare trip into the downtown area known as the Loop. When we approached the parking garage, we saw what appeared to be two long lines to enter, and so we pulled into the shorter one. Suddenly a beautifully dressed woman whose car was in the other line exited her car and made a beeline for ours, screaming obscenities at us. Apparently we had unknowingly cut into a line. We tried to apologize, but she kept on screaming; we tried to placate, but she would have none of it. I felt sick for hours as her abusive anger and obscene language echoed in my head.

I wish I could say that God's children don't lose control like that. But I've observed them. And so have you. Knock on any door on any day of the week. When the door opens, enter like the invisible Shadow and observe the painful scenes resulting from a loss of self-control.

A teenage girl hangs up the phone in tears after her best friend lays into her over a misunderstanding.

A despondent husband sits hunched over a desk, his face in his hands, unpaid bills piled high because his wife can't control her spending.

A wife runs to her bedroom to escape her husband's angry voice swearing at her. She murmurs to herself bitterly, "And he says he's a Christian!"

A man is passed out on a couch because he can't control his drinking.

All these scenes—and many more—are evidence of the painful consequences of a lack of self-control.

GOD SAYS, "GET A GRIP!"

In Titus 2:5 Paul commands older women to teach younger women to be self-controlled (*sophron*). *Sophron* in the original language means "of a sound mind, self-controlled, soberminded."[1] In the *King James Version sophron* is translated as "discreet"; in the Phillips translation it's "sensible"; and in the *New English Bible* it's "temperate." The view from the top of this character trait looks different in every direction. "Discreet" and "temperate" don't seem that similar; "sensible" doesn't necessarily make you think of "self-controlled." But Vine's dictionary says the word means "sound judgment" and describes it as that "habitual inner self-government, with its constant rein on all the passions and desires, which would hinder the temptation to these from arising, or at all events from arising in such strength as would overbear the check and barriers."[2]

With this definition in mind, take a minute and think with me about some synonyms for self-control. Here is a partial list:

- self-discipline
- composure

146

- levelheadedness
- soberness
- stability
- patience
- temperance
- forbearance

A self-controlled person is:

- prudent
- careful
- circumspect
- moderate
- restrained

As I look at these lists of words, I realize they seem a bit old-fashioned. Most have dropped out of our vocabulary. Oh, we talk about a person being a "moderate" politically or about a "temperate" climate, but when was the last time you heard a person described as "circumspect" or "restrained"? When you really want to compliment a person, can you imagine saying, "You know, I really respect you for your moderation, prudence, forbearance, soberness, and temperance"? You'd get some strange looks! And yet, the Holy Spirit directed Paul to single out self-control as one of the essential qualities for godly women to develop.

In a world that tells us that to repress any emotion (whether rage or ecstasy) is to be dishonest, where to be sensible is to be stuffy, where to be restrained is to be dull—to be self-controlled is, well, radical. And yet the lack of self-control has led to unrestrained behavior and a nightmare maze of drugs, shootings, irresponsible sex, and corrupt behavior. Blatant examples abound—in supermarkets, malls, and on the street. Jack and I were sickened, but not surprised, to discover the other night that every car parked on our street had a window smashed in. Another night, someone thought it fun to drive by and batter each mailbox. To display a carved pumpkin on Halloween is tantamount to an invitation to smash it on the driveway.

Our city was horrified recently when a fifty-five-year-old, retired military man shot and killed a teenage boy who had been tailgating him. Both were angry when the older man motioned for the boy to pull over. When the teenager approached the older man's car and punched him through the open window, the older man, who had a loaded gun in his lap, shot and killed him. Even more shocking to most in our town was that the older man went free!

God advocates the exact opposite of unrestrained behavior. God says clearly, "Get a grip!"

WHAT SELF-CONTROL LOOKS LIKE

Titus 2:11-12 gives us the essence of self-control: "For the grace of God that brings salvation has appeared to all men. It [grace] teaches us to say "No" to ungodliness and worldly passions, and to live self-controlled, upright and godly lives in this present age."

How do we have self-control? Through God's grace. (Aren't you glad you don't have to crank it up all by yourself?) What is self-control? Saying no to ungodliness and worldly passions, and living self-controlled, upright, and godly lives. Godly self-control includes the following elements.

Thinking Straight

Clear-mindedness and self-control are coupled in 1 Peter 4:7, which says, "The end of all things is near. Therefore be clear minded and self-controlled so that you can pray," and in 1 Peter 1:13, which says, "Therefore, prepare your minds for action; be self-controlled; set your hope fully on the grace to be given you when Jesus Christ is revealed."

Self-control starts in the *mind*. Stop a minute and consider the kinds of thoughts you have the most difficulty controlling. Are they thoughts of jealousy, envy, revenge, anger, or . . . ? I have difficulty not replaying unpleasant conversations in my mind and wishing I'd handled them differently. You know what I mean: *Boy, when she said that, I should have said . . . then she would have said . . . and I would have responded . . .*

I remember one woman who told me that, among other things, she didn't like the way I laughed. She thought I laughed too loudly and that I did it to call attention to myself. She had misjudged my motives, and for weeks I found myself replaying that conversation in my head. I had to spend much time in prayer in order to have the self-control it took to stop.

Acting Right

As a young child, I had out-of-control temper tantrums. I would scream and hit my head against the wall. Mother's response was to put me in my room until I got a grip. I was allowed to pound up the stairs, slam a few connecting doors, throw myself on my bed, and cry. I was not allowed to scream at people, hit anyone, or yell, "I hate you!" I didn't realize it at the time, but Mother was teaching me self-control. She was teaching me something of what it means to "act right." Godly self-control is evidenced by constraint of speech, thoughts, and behavior.

Avoiding Excesses

Our world takes almost everything to excess. We know about Alcoholics Anonymous, Gamblers Anonymous, Overeaters Anonymous, but we tend to overlook the times we work obsessively, play sports fanatically, and watch television excessively. Moderation is rarely preached or taught, yet moderation is a big part of self-control. Learning it isn't easy.

Parents can help instill self-control in their children before their kids get entrenched in excess. I have a friend who taught his children both selection skills and moderation in television when he told them they had to read two hours for every thirty minutes of preselected television programs. Today his children are great readers and watch very little television.

EXAMINE YOURSELF

There's a proverb in the business world that says the man who takes no inventories eventually becomes bankrupt. A good hard look at our own self-control is necessary—and it's important to have the right measuring stick.

The story is told of a little boy who came to his mother one day and said, "Mother, guess what! I'm eight feet four inches tall!" When his mother looked into it, she found he was using a six-inch ruler; he was actually four feet two inches tall. If we aren't careful, we measure ourselves by one another or by our own distorted views of ourselves instead of by the Word of God.

When I take a look at my self-control on serene, hassle-free days, I may see myself as patient and calm and give myself a pat on the back:

Hey, great self-control, lady! But then a day of frustrating and adverse circumstances comes along, and suddenly I'm face to face with reality. I'm impatient. I may even lose it. (Yes, me.) It's then I remember what a friend said when asked if a particular person who worked for him had a good attitude: "I'm not sure if it is a good attitude or just an *untested* attitude."

Bad days test our self-control. A godly woman once told me, "Pressure brings the scum of my life to the top. My prayer is that I won't stir that scum back in but allow God to skim it off." Pressure, unpleasant circumstances, discouraging situations, unfulfilled expectations, sickness, family problems, and a million other things in life bring up the sludge of our lives so it's visible to all. We are tempted to ignore, hide, or excuse our lack of self-control, but until we recognize it for what it is and confess it and ask God to forgive us and change us, our lack of self-control will continue to pop up whenever it's challenged by frustration or adversity. Only God is able to skim it from our lives.

IDENTIFY ROLE MODELS

We aren't born with self-control; we have to learn it. Perhaps the best way to learn it is to become close to someone who exhibits it. When the world's greatest expert in identifying counterfeit money was asked how he became so adept, he didn't say he spent countless hours looking at various examples of counterfeit money. Instead he said, "By spending months and years examining *the real thing*." We learn self-control the same way. My parents exemplified the godly character trait of self-control. A few times in my life I saw Dad literally white with anger, but he never raised his voice, lashed out physically, or said things he didn't mean. However, Dad had a phleg-matic personality, so perhaps this behavior came more naturally to him. Mom's personality was quite the opposite; she was artistic, tem-peramental, and creative. Yet she demonstrated self-control in her life as well.

My maternal grandmother made her home with us for almost twenty years, and in her later years she became withdrawn, occasion-ally depressed, and somewhat senile. There were times when she got on the nerves of the whole family. We children were not above snap-ping at her in anger or frustration, but I can't remember Mother ever speaking to her that way. I'm sure Mother spent extra hours with the Lord over this, but she evidenced self-control in her speech and ac-tions.

Who do you know who has self-control? Identify an older woman you've observed who is moderate in her lifestyle, discreet (knows when to speak and when to keep silent), and keeps negative emotions under control. Watch closely how this woman behaves, and then ask her to spend some time with you and tell you what has helped her learn self-control.

When I think of self-controlled people, David in the Old Testa-ment immediately comes to mind. (Of course, he demonstrated dra-matic *lapses* of self-control, too, but Scripture teaches that most of his life was spent as a man after God's heart.) King Saul tried to kill David many times—three times by throwing his spear at him when he'd asked David to play the harp for him (1 Samuel 18:10-11; 19:9-10); then by sending him into the heat of battle (1 Samuel 18:18-25); and even by instructing his attendants and his son Jonathan to murder David (19:1). Yet when David had opportunities for revenge, he wouldn't take them.

Saul pursued David relentlessly with the express purpose of killing him, and yet when Saul went into the cave in which David was hiding, all David did was cut off a corner of his robe (1 Samuel 24). Another time, David went into Saul's camp, and while Saul was sleeping, took Saul's spear and water jug; but David wouldn't let Abishai, his companion, kill Saul. "But the LORD forbid that I should lay a hand on the LORD's anointed," David said (26:11).

When your natural desire is to give way to unbridled emotion but your mind and spirit refuse to give in to the desire, that, my friend, is self-control. You don't have to strive for it by yourself. Philippians 4:13 promises, "I can do everything through him who gives me strength." And that includes demonstrating self-control.

Hallelujah!

 *Making Biblical Truth Yours*

Character qualities such as self-control can be elusive—hard to get our teeth into, chew on, and develop. However, one concrete thing we can do is a topical study of the characteristic we want to exemplify.

HOW TO DO A TOPICAL STUDY

1. In a good concordance *look up ten to twenty-five verses* where the word *self-control* is used. A concordance gives you a part of the verse so you don't have to waste time looking up the verses that might not be helpful. Write out the relevant verses in full.

2. *Outline the verses* you've looked up. If you get stuck in outlining, you can usually use *who, what, where, when,* and *how* to focus your study. In the case of *self-control*, you could use: *what* is self-control (use a dictionary or Bible dictionary), *who* should be self-controlled, *where* (or in what areas of life) should self-control be exercised, and *how* does one practice self-control?

3. *Write down some examples* you've witnessed of the characteristic you're studying, or some expanded thoughts from commentaries.

4. *Make a personal application.* As you study, pray about which verse God would have you focus on and work on, and then do a written personal application on that verse.

Next, study self-control by conducting some *verse studies*. Set aside several weeks and study no more than two or three verses per week. Here are some to start with:

- 1 Timothy 3:11
- Galatians 5:22-24
- Proverbs 25:28
- 1 Thessalonians 5:8
- 1 Peter 1:13-16
- 1 Peter 4:7-8
- 1 Peter 5:6-9

When you finish these verses, look up in a concordance ten more verses that speak to self-control (you may also have to look up words like *discipline* or *temperate*). Then outline these verses. Write down any questions you have.

CHAPTER ELEVEN

Being Pure

In February 1982, the world's largest offshore oil exploration rig was stationed 160 miles off the east coast of Newfoundland. More than thirty stories high, the Ocean Ranger was made to withstand eighty-knot winds and thirty-five-foot seas. It was virtually indestructible.

When a stormy nor'easter whipped up one night, no one seemed alarmed. They had been through the worst storms the Grand Banks had to offer. When an exceptionally large wave broke a window in the control room and short-circuited a switch, no one seemed to notice. What they didn't know was that this tiny switch was causing one of the valves in the giant pier-like stilts, which kept the Ocean Ranger up, to open and fill with water. By the time the first Mayday was sounded on Monday morning, the Ranger was already listing badly, and the seas were up to sixty feet. Soon all eighty-four crew members were dead—all because no one noticed that a little switch short-circuited.

It seems today that the whole world is out to force the little switches of our lives open with the express purpose of destroying us, especially in the area of purity. Being pure is one of the three character traits singled out in Titus 2 for women to have in their lives. This trait may be the most difficult of all to cultivate and maintain.

Before we get down to the specifics of purity we need to look at where purity fits into the bigger picture of righteousness. The Bible's description of a godly person boggles my mind. When I read of the Proverbs 31 woman, I feel hopelessly inept. I grimace when I read 1 Peter 3:4 and find that a godly wife is one who has a gentle and quiet spirit—something of great worth in the sight of God. And I stand absolutely mute and helpless when I read Ephesians 5:1, which says, "Be imitators of God, therefore, as dearly loved children." When I was younger, I tried to squeeze my eyes shut and mentally jump over such impossible verses, hoping God wouldn't notice. But in trying to skip over certain commands, I'd find myself in even hotter water. The scenario went something like this:

I'd read a command like "be imitators of God" and exclaim, "Impossible!" as I took a running start to leap over it.

Plop! I'd land right where it says, "Live as children of light (for the fruit of the light consists in all goodness, righteousness and truth) and find out what pleases the Lord" (Ephesians 5:8-10).

Oh, my goodness! How in the world . . . ?

Sometimes I'd try to jump over whole chapters. But I really did want to be an obedient child of the King. Something else had to be done. So I gritted my teeth and labored back to the start of Ephesians, chapter 4. Suddenly I realized it described the practical working out of the "biggie" in 5:1. Phrases stood out—"Live a life worthy of the calling you have received," "be completely humble and gentle," "be patient, bearing with one another in love" (4:1-2)—all describing what being an imitator of God really is. If I imitate God, then my life will be characterized by reverence, obedience, and gentleness—and something else: purity (5:3-5).

But I'm afraid I'm not very good at imitating God. Truthfully, as the command to imitate God stared me down, I tried my best to wiggle out from under it.

Do you ever argue with yourself? I do. And this was one of those times. I said to me, *Hey, now, wait a minute. In Christ I have met all God's requirements for righteousness. In him I am pure. Romans 8:2-4 says that God set me free from the law of sin and death by "sending his own Son in the likeness of sinful man to be a sin offering. And so he condemned sin in sinful man, in order that the righteous requirements of the law might be fully met in us." So when God looks at me, He sees me perfect because I'm cleansed from all sin. I'm "wrapped in Jesus." In a real sense, then, I already am imitating God. Well, positionally, anyhow.*

But me argued back with I: *Who are you kidding? You may be perfect in my eyes because of Christ, but what are you actually?"*

Don't bring that up, I grumbled.

Think about it!

Okay, I admit it. Actually, I'm pretty repugnant. My old nature still looms big, and the world tugs and pulls. Then there's the flesh and the Devil. Yeah, I guess I'd have to admit: Practically and actually, I'm a mess!"

"Now that that's settled, let's take a serious look at this business of being an imitator of God.

And so Ephesians became my source book to teach me that God is in the business of practically making me into what positionally He declares me to be. (Hope you got that!) My thoughts said, *Father, help! I need to know what You really mean when You say to be an imitator of You, and I need to know how in the world I can do that.*

My Father said, "Listen." Then He showed me the outline and filled in the details. And He didn't leave much out. It had been there in His Book all the time.

I'm to be an imitator of God, which means being a child of the light in all goodness, righteousness, and truth. Get that? *All* goodness. *All* righteousness. *All* truth. That's the general principle.

And the details follow: I'm to be *completely* humble and gentle (4:2); make *every* effort to keep the unity of the Spirit through the bond of peace (4:3); grow up to be mature in Christ (4:15); put on a new self, created to be like God in true righteousness and holiness (4:24); be kind, compassionate, totally forgiving (4:32); and give thanks for everything (5:20). That's all! And those are just the positive characteristics God wants in my life. The list is just as long for the things He doesn't want in my life—and many of those have to do with purity. I'm not to let *any* unwholesome talk come out of my mouth (4:29) or grieve the Spirit (4:30). I'm to get rid of *all* bitterness, rage, anger, brawling, slander, every form of malice, and have nothing to do with the unfruitful works of darkness (5:11).

Enough already! I thought. But there's more. God says there shouldn't be even a *hint* of sexual immorality in my life or any kind of impurity or greed or anything that *suggests* that things are improper or out of place.

"Whew! That blows me away, Lord. I wish You hadn't been quite so detailed, but okay. That takes care of *what* You mean. (And is more than I'll ever be able to put into practice.) But *how* can I even begin to imitate You like that, Lord?"

The Father said, "Look again." And I searched the book with increasing wonder and found I don't have to do it by myself. God has *redeemed* me: "In him we have redemption through his blood, the forgiveness of sins, in accordance with the riches of God's grace that he lavished on us with all wisdom and understanding" (Ephesians 1:7-8). He has reached out to me (and the human race) and paid the penalty for my sin so I can be forgiven and restored. When I am redeemed, the Holy Spirit indwells me and becomes my powerful Helper to live the way God wants me to live.

God also *transforms* me when I "put off" my old self and "put on" my new self in the attitude of my mind (4:22-24). This new self is created to be like God in true righteousness and holiness.

Finally, God *conforms* me to His image (Romans 8:29), which is a process that happens when I'm open to Him and to every circumstance He brings into my life.

An overweight woman went to a diet center one day, and after being weighed in, she stood in front of a mirror while the person in charge outlined a shape several inches slimmer and explained, "Our goal is, at the end of ten weeks, to have you fit into this outline."

The woman worked hard. She dieted and exercised, and every week she came into the center and stood in front of the mirror. But she couldn't quite fit into the outlined proportion. So she went home and worked even harder.

Then one day when she stood in front of the mirror, she was *conformed* to its image!

It took me awhile to understand the concept of being an "imitator," which means to copy, duplicate, emulate, mimic, and follow. When our granddaughter Sunny was two and a half, she puppy-dogged her older brother Eric, five and a half, all day long. Everything he did, she did. Everywhere he went, she went. Finally at supper, Eric spread his arms wide and, brimming tears of frustration, announced to all, "Sunny does everything I do . . . only louder!"

Sunny's behavior didn't make Eric happy, but our imitating God would make Him very happy indeed. Wouldn't it be wonderful if people, observing Christians, could say, "They do everything Christ did . . . only louder—because there are more of them"?

That's my goal. To be conformed to the image of Christ by imitating God. To be reverent and pure in the way I live.

WHAT DOES PURITY LOOK LIKE?

"To the pure, all things are pure, but to those who are corrupted and do not believe, nothing is pure. In fact, both their minds and consciences are corrupted. They claim to know God, but by their actions they deny him. They are detestable, disobedient and unfit for doing anything good" (Titus 1:15-16).

According to this verse, purity means we are to be pure in mind, conscience, and actions.

Pure in Mind
Our thinking is warped and corrupted just from living in the world and unconsciously embracing the lies our world tells us. Recently I listened to a woman . . . and ached inside.

"I've been on antidepressants for many years," she said. "Most of what I earn goes to my therapists, and my kids have begun to resent that, but I need to go twice a week or I wouldn't make it. The therapist I had for four years didn't help me much, but the one I'm seeing now is. The medication makes me sleepy and dull, but I need it. I'm grateful my boss understands. He's become a Jesus-figure to me."

For this woman, her therapist was Wisdom, her counselor Knowledge. Her medication became the "lifter of her head" (or mood), and her boss was the Jesus-figure in her life.

There seems to be a pervasive attitude in Christendom today that says hang-ups are to be treated by psychologists, hurts solved by therapy groups, and satanic attacks met with courses in spiritual warfare. Christ's wisdom is beneficial, sure, but more help than that is needed for real deliverance. What happened to the sufficiency of Christ?

The apostle Paul clearly stated his purpose in helping and discipling people this way:

> My purpose is that they may be encouraged in heart and united in love, so that they may have the full riches of complete understanding, in order that they may know the mystery of God, namely, Christ in whom are hidden all the treasures of wisdom and knowledge. (Colossians 2:2-3)

Following the statement of his purpose, Paul wrote some grave warnings: We aren't to be deceived by "fine-sounding arguments" (v. 4) or to be taken "captive through hollow and deceptive philosophy, which depends on human tradition and the basic principles of this world rather than on Christ" (v. 8). He cautions that if we aren't careful, we lose "connection with the Head" (v. 19).

We need to be *immersed* in Christ. He is our life. He is our glory. He is, in fact, everything. It seems to me that being consumed with Christ could take care of our dysfunctional pasts, put present difficulties into perspective, and help us see life from His perspective rather than our own.

If we are *pure in mind*, Christ says, we will not take in the world's lies. "It is the thought-life that defiles you. For from within, out of a person's heart, come evil thoughts, sexual immorality, theft, murder, adultery, greed, wickedness, deceit, eagerness for lustful pleasure, envy, slander, pride, and foolishness. All these vile things come from within; they are what defile you and make you unacceptable to God" (Mark 7:20-23, NLT).

Since our thought-lives can defile us and cause impurity, we need to guard our thoughts with all diligence. What we allow to be taken in through our eyes goes into our minds, sits there, and very quickly starts to smell. Yet many of us have few convictions about the types of movies we see, books we read, or activities in which we participate. And then we wonder why our thoughts aren't pure.

One morning I read in Psalm 101, "I will walk in my house with blameless heart. I will set before my eyes no vile thing" (2-3). I started to read on, but the Lord brought my eyes back to that verse—several times. I protested, "Come on now. I don't have vile things in my house." But the voice of the Spirit wouldn't let me off that easy. He brought to mind a few of the programs I'd been watching on television, an assortment of books and magazines I sometimes perused, even some of the gossip I listened to. And I realized that some things needed cleansing from the closet in my soul.

I agonized over the application God wanted me to make in my life and finally decided that if a book had a detailed sex scene, I'd throw it in the wastebasket—even if I'd paid good money for it. (No use even giving it to Goodwill; if I shouldn't read it, it wouldn't benefit anyone else, would it?) I stopped mindlessly flipping on the television; instead, I marked the programs in the *TV Guide* that I felt were okay to watch and disciplined myself not to turn on the set at other times.

We need a sensitivity to the Holy Spirit in order not to allow the world's garbage to be tossed onto the floor of our lives. To be pure, some of us will have to clean house!

Pure in Conscience

Periodically I need to take a microscope to my life for this one. Not only does my mind need to be pure, but my conscience needs to be pure as well. In Acts 24:16 Paul said, "So I strive always to keep my conscience clear before God and man."

A person who is pure isn't devious, suspicious, doubting, or corrupted. She is guileless and believes that others' motives are good until proven otherwise. Because so many of us have become numb to sin by our walk in this world, one of the most important things we can pray continually is, "Lord, make me . . . keep me . . . sensitive to sin."

One day years ago as I answered the phone, an acquaintance's voice came over the wire. "I called to apologize and ask your forgiveness," she said.

Mystified, I replied, "For what?"

"The other night when my husband and I came into a meeting and you greeted us, my husband thought I was distant and cold toward you, and I want to apologize."

I still remember the awe I felt. I hadn't noticed her being "distant and cold." But I was touched by her willingness to humble herself and ask forgiveness. It's a lesson that has stuck with me over the years and is a part of keeping a heart pure in conscience.

Have you ever had the Lord convict you about something you need to ask forgiveness for, either from Him or a person? I can't count the number of times God has "pricked my conscience" until I've made a difficult phone call, asked for a face-to-face appointment with someone, or written a letter of apology for something I've said or done that was hurtful. I've had to say, "I was wrong. I'm sorry. Will you forgive me?"—nine words that are critical for us to use often if we want to be pure in conscience.

Pure in Deeds

When we think of someone as pure, our first thought is usually of sexual purity—and that's biblical. In fact, there are no gray areas on this subject. Paul says,

> It is God's will that you should be sanctified: that you should avoid sexual immorality; that each of you should learn to control his own body in a way that is holy and honorable, not in passionate lust. . . . For God did not call us to be impure, but to live a holy life. (1 Thessalonians 4:3-5,7)
>
> Flee from sexual immorality. All other sins a man commits are outside his body, but he who sins sexually sins against his own body. Do you not know that your body is a temple of the Holy Spirit, who is in you, whom you have received from God? You are not your own; you were bought at a price. Therefore honor God with your body. (1 Corinthians 6:18-20)

It's hard not to become blasé about sexual sin when television and the media bombard us with the message that sex outside marriage is okay. The world plays mind games with us and brainwashes us into thinking that it's no big deal to have premarital sex or to be unfaithful to our spouse or to have a child out of wedlock. However, God's commandments are clear: "Flee from sexual immorality." And He doesn't stop there. He says that there shouldn't even be a *hint* of it in our lives—including crude jokes and innuendoes.

They say what goes around comes around, and dress styles are a case in point. I've heard that skirt lengths go up and down with the stock market, but whatever affects them, when Lynn was in her teens, skirts were way up. She and I had talked at length about how short skirts could cause a guy's thoughts to zero in on what he shouldn't be thinking about, but she didn't really hear me until a youth leader she respected got all the girls in the group together and told it like it was. He said, "Do you think the guys think it's accidental when your skirt hitches up so your underwear shows? Do you know why some guys who want to keep their thoughts pure won't go swimming when girls are in the pool? Do you know what a guy's first thought is when he takes you out on a date?" When Lynn got home from that meeting, her eyes were wide and her heart convicted.

One man commented recently, "We are not even safe [from impurity] in our own homes, so keeping alert concerning purity and holiness is vital." He was referring not only to the things on television and rented videos but also to the pornographic photographs and discussions available today via the Internet.

"Pure in deeds" encompasses a host of things besides sexual purity, of course, though the Bible zeros in on this aspect of purity most frequently. More and more we're hearing about unhealthy relationships developed through chat rooms and great amounts of time spent "surfing the Net." All of these certainly lure us away from a pure devotion to Christ.

HOW TO BECOME PURE

Remember, my friend, you are pure *in Christ*. And it is only Christ who continues to purify you. Christ is your head (Colossians 2:19), and if you allow your Head control, you won't have to worry about 1,001 different commands. You'll need to be concerned about only one: to obey what your Head tells you to do.

In order to hear what He tells you, you need to absorb God's Word, especially through personal application. When David cried out to God, "How can a young man keep his way pure?" the answer he came up with was, "by living according to your word" (Psalm 119:9). David gave us the key to doing that by declaring, "I have hidden your word in my heart that I might not sin against you" (v. 11).

A friend told us of a serviceman, a new believer, who was concerned about his swearing. He said, "I'm able to control the swearing when I'm awake, but I talk in my sleep, and the men in the barracks tell me I swear in my sleep. What can I do?"

The man who had led this serviceman to Christ suggested that he begin memorizing Scripture regularly, which he did. Soon the men in the barracks heard him quoting verses of Scripture in his sleep!

Psalm 51:10 needs to be our constant prayer: "Create in me a pure heart, O God, [create means 'from scratch—out of nothing,' which is what we often need] and renew a steadfast spirit within me [renew means to make new, begin again]." When we come to the Father helpless and in need, He acts on our behalf. He has purified us by sending us His Son, and He gives us His Spirit to work in us to do his will—which includes living pure lives as we . . .

saturate ourselves in His Word . . .
seek to obey His commands . . .
and sit at the feet of Jesus.

 *Making Biblical Truth Yours*

Try these *verse studies:*

- Philippians 4:8
- 1 Timothy 5:22
- 1 Timothy 6:11-12
- James 1:27
- 1 John 3:1-3

Next, do a *topical study* on the word *pure*. (You might want to use some of the verses in this chapter.)

Meditate on 1 Peter 3:16: "Keeping a clear conscience, so that those who speak maliciously against your good behavior in Christ may be ashamed of their slander." Read the context of this verse. How should this affect your behavior toward those people who don't know Christ? Think of a way you've obeyed this verse and one way you haven't.

Finally, *memorize* four verses on purity during the next two weeks.

CHAPTER TWELVE

Being Kind

"I'm not going down for breakfast," I quavered. "Please go on without me."

Jack looked at me for a long moment and then said, "Okay. I understand." As he leaned over to kiss me, guilt stabbed my heart. It wasn't fair that he had to face the situation alone. But my eyes were puffy from crying, and I just couldn't face the group gathered in the dining room after the men had criticized Jack so cruelly the evening before. The tears welled up again as I packed our suitcases and waited for Jack to return so we could, at last, get in the car and scurry home.

When I opened the door of our room a short time later, I noticed a small paper bag on the doorstep. In it was a Snickers bar and a note from one of the wives of the men involved, expressing her sympathy for how she knew I must be feeling. I've never forgotten her kindness.

There are some God-blessed people who are born with a gentle and kind nature. Others develop this quality because they've been raised in a home where kindness is taught by example and words. But

169

those who have neither a naturally kind nature nor an exemplary background can have hope. God can "grow" the quality of kindness in us if we open our hearts and allow Him free access to our lives. We can *learn* how to be kind in both speech and action.

The attribute of kindness is one of the fruits of the Holy Spirit listed in Galatians 5:22-23. Four out of the nine fruits listed are reiterated as characteristics that should be taught specifically to women: love, self-control, kindness (gentleness, in some translations), and purity (or goodness).

To me, kindness is the overflow and outgrowth of love. In fact, I've wondered if the punctuation of Galatians 5:22-23 wouldn't still be accurate if we put in a colon after "love," making it read: "But the fruit of the Spirit is love: [which manifests itself in] joy, peace, patience, kindness, goodness, faithfulness, gentleness and self-control." It seems to me that if we have the sort of love we should, we would manifest patience, kindness, and all the rest.

Kindness is identified as one of the attributes of love in 1 Corinthians 13:4. God commands us to "be kind and compassionate" (Ephesians 4:32) and to "always try to be kind to each other" (1 Thessalonians 5:15). Second Timothy 2:24 insists that we be kind to *everyone*.

Sonja and I were sitting in the breakfast nook discussing this subject over a cup of coffee when Sonja made a statement that needs to be mulled over and absorbed. "Kindness," she said "is a gift you *choose* to give someone." She went on to say that kindness goes beyond being fair or just. We may do or say something that is just or true, but we still have an obligation to be kind at the same time.

And how do we do that? Kindness flows through our lives by what we say and how we say it, and what we do and how we do it.

WHAT WE SAY AND HOW WE SAY IT

While God is the true lifter of our heads (Psalm 3:3, KJV), He often uses our words to cheer the hearts of His people. Kind words make light hearts. Proverbs 12:25 says, "An anxious heart weighs a man down, but a kind word cheers him up."

At a time in our lives when we had no money for a needed winter coat, Mom Mayhall, having just moved to California, gave me her beige wool coat. Because beige makes me look like a dead fish, I spent a precious eight dollars to have the coat dyed bright blue.

One day on my way to town I felt especially discouraged and defeated about life, finances, and having to wear my mother-in-law's dyed coat. Suddenly a woman passing me on the other side of a wide sidewalk strode diagonally across to me, smiled, and said, "I just had to tell you what a beautiful coat you have!"

Suddenly the world seemed newly sun washed. I looked down and thought, *You know, it is a pretty coat.* And I thanked the Lord both for the coat and for my thoughtful mother-in-law.

I wonder, friend, how many times you and I have missed opportunities to be kind through offering an encouraging word to someone—husband, child, friend, or stranger. Scripture says that we are not to withhold good from those who deserve it, when it is within our power to act (Proverbs 3:27), and yet, often we "withhold" a kind word.

One of the most unkind habits of speech is something of which we are often unaware. Much of today's humor is based on it, and we hear it on almost every sitcom. Its name is *sarcasm*. Sarcasm, according to the dictionary, is "a taunting, sneering, cutting, or caustic remark; gibe or jeer, generally ironical and implies an intent to hurt." Someone said that what is scary about our nation is not so much what we do but what we laugh at. We begin to think that sarcasm is not only normal but the only way to jest, and we begin to play the game "Can you top this?"

I read these two stories not long ago:

> She came into the room with her scalp bristling in pink plastic curlers. He said, "What happened to your hair?"
>
> She said, "I set it."
>
> He said, "What time does it go off?"

And in contrast:

> Coming a bit early, the young man caught his date with half her hair up in rollers, the other half every which way. Embarrassed, but trying to make the best of the situation, she gave him a wide smile and chirped, "Well, what do you think?"
>
> He paused a moment, returned her grin, and said, "I think it looks like something beautiful is about to happen!"

I laughed at both stories. But only one is kind.

WHAT WE DO AND HOW WE DO IT

Deeds of kindness come in the form of a smile, an encouraging word, a scrawled note, a timely phone call . . . and acts. Lots and lots of acts such as these:

Sunshine broke through a rather routine, humdrum day, when a new friend knocked on my door with four, freshly baked cinnamon rolls and a cheery, "Hi, just baked these and thought you and Jack might like some."

Waiting in a hospital room for news on shoulder surgery for Jack was made less painful when my brother-in-law slipped into the waiting room and kept me company until the doctor appeared at the door.

Last week I received a humorous card from someone I didn't know. The front had a bear in a bathtub full of suds and said, "When life gets too hectic, I've always found that a nice, hot bath can solve most problems." Inside it said, "I've been in here since last Thursday." The woman wrote that the card had reminded her of an illustration I'd shared, and it cheered me as I laughed.

Kindness is thoughtfulness that stems from a tender heart, empathy born of compassion, mercy given with consideration. Kindness expects no return on its investment.

When a family of missionaries visited our little church, as usual Mom and Dad invited them to be our guests. But a glitch in visas became a hitch in their return to the field, and the weekend extended into a month as we shared our home with them. Mom extended herself to them—and became a lasting friend. She reached out to them with no thought of what she'd get in return.

Proverbs 14:21 says, "Blessed is he who is kind to the needy." People with a variety of needs—physical, emotional, spiritual—surround us. Often when there is a death in a family we say, "If there's anything I can do, just let me know"—but they rarely do. I heard of a man who slipped into the house of bereaved family friends and polished every pair of shoes he could find so they would be ready for the funeral the next day. Another friend came and cleaned their house from top to bottom. Those were special acts of kindness to people in need.

We are to be kind even to our enemies. Yes, our enemies. In Luke 6:35 Christ says, "But love your enemies, do good to them, and lend to them without expecting to get anything back. Then your reward will be great, and you will be sons of the Most High, because he is kind to the ungrateful and wicked." Our motivation to be kind is because God is kind.

You've heard the saying, "Familiarity breeds contempt." Well, I think familiarity also breeds unkindness. One friend said, "Bible study groups would have far fewer problems if the members constantly reminded themselves to be kind." She went on to say that women are often unkind to each other by talking behind each other's backs or snubbing each other. When I asked what she meant by "snubbing," she said women in her Bible study sometimes deliberately left out a person when the group got together for lunch after the study, or they excluded various individuals when communicating important news, or even left them out of a prayer chain. To this woman, these forms of snubbing rated a top spot on the "most cruel" list.

I looked up *snub* in the dictionary. It means "to treat with scorn, contempt, disdain; behave coldly toward; slight or ignore." Slighting, ignoring, or treating someone with disdain is not kind. And "kindness is a gift you give someone."

How to Develop the Quality of Kindness

Perhaps the first thing to do is to take a good, hard, long look at your own life right now. Put a mental tape recorder in some corner of your soul to record your words and actions. Ask God for the ability to mentally stand outside of your life and observe.

One day I decided I'd listen to myself while I was driving alone. I have to admit I was appalled. My monologue sounded something like this:

(at a stoplight) "Come on, lady. It's the only shade of green we've got."

(at a corner) "Mister, don't you know what turn signals are for?"

(at a stop sign) "Would you please *move it*, buddy?"

And on and on I went. True, nobody heard me. But God heard. And He quickly showed me that my mutterings were not only impatient; they were unkind.

How do we learn to be kind—a quality that doesn't come naturally to most of us?

Study the Subject

Doing a study of how God is kind may be of help. Remember, we are to imitate Him, so it's important to take a long look at One who is kind beyond our comprehension.

Listen to Ephesians 2:6-7: "And God raised us up with Christ and seated us with him in the heavenly realms in Christ Jesus, in order that in the coming ages he might show the incomparable riches of his grace, expressed in his kindness to us in Christ Jesus."

Romans 11:22 says, "Consider therefore the kindness and sternness of God: sternness to those who fell, but kindness to you, provided that you continue in his kindness."

Jeremiah 9:23 declares, "This is what the LORD says: 'Let not the wise man boast of his wisdom or the strong man boast of his strength or the rich man boast of his riches, but let him who boasts boast about this: that he understands and knows me, that I am the LORD, who exercises kindness, justice and righteousness on earth, for in these I delight.'"

I love that phrase "God *exercises* kindness." God not only embodies kindness, but He exercises it! He sets out deliberately to be kind. So must we.

Pray for the Ability to Be Kind

To learn a character trait such as kindness takes more than our concentrated effort; it takes the power of God. We need to put that specific needed quality at the top of our prayer lists. I said "specific." Don't just pray to be kind—that's too general. Pray that you'll be kind even as you discipline your children, even when you're tired, even when you feel taken advantage of. A good way to start praying is by asking God to make you alert to particular areas in your life where it's easy for you to be unkind. With family members who we know will love and accept us "no matter what," we tend to let our hair down and say things we wouldn't consider saying to a stranger.

One friend of mine asks God for a "year verse" for the quality she feels she needs most in her life. Then she writes it out on a bookmark and puts it in her Bible. Every day as she has her quiet time, she reads the verse and prays over it. She says that while the lessons God brings into her life to teach her that quality are sometimes difficult, her life has been greatly enriched as a result.

You know, it's easy to excuse ourselves, isn't it? When we hurt someone with our unkindness, we often say, "I'm sorry—I just didn't think . . ." (You fill in the blank: I just didn't think that would hurt you. . . . I just didn't think you'd want to be included. . . . I didn't mean it that way. . . .) It's a convenient excuse—but not an acceptable one. God can help us *consider* what we say, think through the results of our actions, and think before we speak. But yes, it does take His help! And I'm sure glad God is patient with me, aren't you?

Ask Others for Help

A further step—if you dare—is to ask for help from those closest to you. Scary? Yes. Humiliating? Surely. But if you're serious about having godly qualities as a part of your character, it may be necessary.

Lynn talks about the "throwaways" people use in conversation—the off-the-cuff statements that give clues about what the person is really thinking or is interested in. If we would pick up on these statements and pursue them, we'd have a wealth of information about the person—or about what he or she might be thinking of us.

A "throwaway" might be a statement like, "There sure are a lot of critical people out there." We could say, "Yes, that's true," and go on to something else—or we could probe a bit deeper and ask questions like, "What do you mean? What do you think makes them that way? What are they critical about? Do you think *I'm* critical?"

Are you wise enough or caring enough to pick up on the "throwaways"? Are you humble enough to pursue a subject that hurts you? Are you eager enough to try anything to improve? I must admit, often I'm not. Oh, sometimes I'll "pick up" with Jack. If he says, "You know, you're too busy," I'll quiz him in depth ("What do you mean? Am I neglecting you? Lynn? The house?"). I'll pick up with Lynn if she says, "You seem a bit distracted." ("Do you think I'm not listening? Not interested?") I'll pick up with Sonja if she says, "You sounded a bit critical there." But do I probe with people I don't know well or people I don't think really know me? I'm inclined to ignore those folks and hope they just go away. I need to be aware of the throwaways and casual statements others make that might help me become more honest with myself. And I need to risk *asking* people close to me to help me see my own blind spots.

Kindness can be learned and developed, and God will give us

the grace to grow in it. Kindness is a vital character trait whether it's expressed by a Snickers and a note left on a doorstep, a kind word about a dyed winter coat, or cinnamon rolls shared by a new friend. Kindness is like balm applied to the wounds and hurts of life.

Making Biblical Truth Yours

This is "observation week"! For the next seven days, keep an eye out for acts of kindness around you—from your husband, children, friends, strangers—or ones you read about. Jot down those acts of kindness. Take a moment to thank the Lord when you see them. Then, as you pray, decide on one deliberate act of kindness to do each day. Keep a list of those, too.

Then do the following *verse studies:*

- Ephesians 4:32
- Proverbs 31:26
- Colossians 3:12
- 1 Timothy 5:10
- Proverbs 11:16

HOW TO DO A TOPICAL STUDY USING THE ACROSTIC T-O-P-I-C-A-L

Do a *topical study* on the word *kind* or *kindness*. We did one kind of topical study when we studied self-control in chapter 10, but let's expand that by using the acrostic T-O-P-I-C-A-L:

T—Title
In this case we can use "Kindness" or "What the Bible Says about Kindness" or "Keys to Kindness."

O—Outline
As you look over your verses, sometimes a natural outline is evident. If not, you can always use *who, what, where, why, when,* and *how.* On the subject of kindness you might have sections like: definition of kindness (dictionary and Bible dictionary); character traits coupled with kindness; the source of kindness (Galatians 5:22-23); who should be kind; examples of kindness; the keys to developing kindness, etc.

P—Problems
Questions will come up as you study the verses. You don't have to have answers to all of them (though other scriptures may shed some light on them), but as you study the verses and have questions or problems understanding, jot them down. *Why is kindness often coupled with self-control? With understanding? Was Christ always kind? If not, why? What are some examples of His not seeming kind?*

I—Illustrations
Often illustrations are from our own experiences, but keep looking for illustrations from Scripture as well. Keep a notebook handy to write down stories you hear in sermons or read in books.

C—Commentaries
Hopefully you'll be able to invest in a good set of commentaries written by godly people who have studied in the original language. You'll be able to look up their thoughts on many subjects and passages.

A—Application

This is the most important step of all, but since the Enemy of our souls doesn't want us to do it, it may be one of the most difficult things to do consistently. An application should be personal, practical, and something you can do *this week*. For instance, if God begins to speak to you about the times you are unkind to your children (e.g., like getting cranky when trying to get supper on the table), ask God for ideas to help you during those times. He might lead you to write out Ephesians 4:32 on a large card and put it above your sink to read every day at that time.

L—List

As you look up and study verses on kindness, no doubt a few will grab your attention. Write these down in a notebook under "Verses for Future Memorization." Read these over every month or so, and choose one to commit to memory.

To complete this chapter's study section, *memorize* four verses on kindness.

CHAPTER THIRTEEN

Practicing Submission

The heavyset woman plunked down next to me in the long row of chairs and, sounding weary and resigned, blurted out, "Well, I want you to know that I've done everything my husband has told me to for one whole month."

I looked at her with surprise, not having a clue as to what prompted this outburst. I didn't recognize the woman, but apparently she knew that sometimes I speak on husband-wife relationships. She was answering a question I'd never asked and assuring me she'd been pretty good at what she supposed was submission.

I thought, *Bless your bones. That is the furthest thing from biblical submission I ever did hear!*

But there was a time when I might have thought the same thing.

When Jack and I married, I assumed submission meant becoming a "yes woman," a blah person who had no personality or opinions of her own, a mindless nonentity. In addition, I thought that if I were to become a submissive wife, Jack would become demanding, selfish, and dictatorial. I wasn't having any of that either! I took the rather common view that marriage was a 50-50 proposition. If Jack would give his 50 percent, I (maybe) would give mine. The only difficulty was we were always fighting about whose turn it was to give the 50 percent! (Years later I learned that to have a successful marriage, both parties need to be willing to give the total 100 percent, all the time.)

As my walk with God deepened and He began to speak to my heart about being submissive, God and I had quite an argument. In fact, we battled over this for several months. First I did a topical study of the verses that commanded me to submit to see if they *really* said that. They did. Then in my Bible-reading program as well as additional study, I tried to find all the scriptural "out's"—incidents in which wives *didn't* submit and either got away with it or were commended for it. I managed to find a few wives who manipulated or deceived, but none were cited as positive examples. In fact, the one who is cited as a godly wife is Sarah in 1 Peter 3 (PH) because she "obeyed Abraham and called him her lord." I took some time to examine what Sarah actually did and was shocked! She lied for Abraham (Genesis 12:1-20, 20:1-17). She actually went to live in the house of another man (twice!) because good, old, brave patriarch Abraham was so afraid he'd be killed (because some powerful person wanted his wife) that he asked Sarah to say she was his sister.

I don't think I'd lie for my husband, nor would anyone today tell me I should. But Sarah did and was held up as a godly example. I fully believe that Sarah was trusting God to keep her from evil—which He did. And she wasn't commended for her lying but for her obedience. Still, it takes some thinking about, doesn't it?

The Bible names only one woman who was wise *not* to obey her husband: Abigail. Her husband, Nabal (a real louse!), wouldn't give food to King David and his men, so David decided to wipe him and his household off the face of the earth. Abigail, without her husband's knowledge or consent, brought David and his men food and presented it to the king with a wise speech, thereby saving the lives of everyone, including her husband (1 Samuel 25). Hearing about the close call, Nabal had a heart attack and died ten days later—and Abigail subsequently married David. That one example brought me small comfort.

I tried hard to make the verse "Wives, submit yourselves unto your own husbands, as unto the Lord" (Ephesians 5:22, KJV) read, "Wives, submit yourselves unto your husbands if they are acting like the Lord." That would be easy! But I couldn't make it say that. Instead, it was saying that in the same free and full way I want to submit to the Lord, I'm to submit to my husband. Tough stuff!

I clearly remember the morning when I finally knelt in my bedroom and said to the Lord, "All right! I give up! I still don't understand the meaning or all the ramifications and results of submission, but that's your business, isn't it, Father? I'm not doing this because Jack said to—or even because he's earned it. I'll do it because You command it. I want to submit to Jack out of obedience to *You*."

What happened astonished me. I don't think I told Jack about my decision—one made up not of dos and don'ts but of an attitude of the heart—a deliberate decision to put myself under Jack's authority, to try not to manipulate or argue to get my own way, to try not to control. The exact opposite of what I thought might happen, happened. Jack started to ask my opinion about *more* things. He became *more* thoughtful and considerate. We became a loving team, pulling together, instead of one obstinate partner hanging back or trying to go another way. I caught a glimpse of the truth of 1 John 5:3, which says, "This is love for God: to obey his commands. And his commands are not *burdensome*" (emphasis mine). God's commands aren't to make things hard for me but to make my life more beautiful, peaceful, and satisfying.

A husband's responsibility to love his wife as Christ loved the church and to lead her as Christ leads the church and looks out for it is awesome. But it seems to me that the responsibility of the wife is equally awesome and formidable, including the command to submit.

I told you that I've had a lot of different ideas on what submission is, and even today, if you and I don't agree on this subject, it won't bother me. I advise you to study the subject personally and come to your own convictions. I beg you, however, to put aside any bias. Start the study by erasing your preconceived ideas, and study directly from Scripture—not others' interpretation of that Scripture (which usually is slanted in one way or another), praying that God will show you *His* truth.

WHAT IS BIBLICAL SUBMISSION?

Many people have strange ideas about submission. One woman told me in the presence of her spouse, "Submission for me is never expressing a negative thought to my husband." Her husband responded, "But I *want* her to! I know she could be my best constructive critic, but she refuses to critique even when I ask her to."

Scripture tells us to "admonish one another with all wisdom" (Colossians 3:16); "[speak] the truth in love" (Ephesians 4:15); "if someone is caught in a sin, you who are spiritual should restore him gently" (Galatians 6:1). These commands are directed at every Christian in the body of Christ, including husbands and wives. Granted, there is a time and place for "admonishing," for voicing negatives. And there should be fifty positives for every negative spoken in a marriage so the atmosphere will be positive rather than critical. But for a wife (who knows her husband better than anyone else in the world) to withhold her observations from her husband, even when they are negative, is a great disservice to him.

Another wife said that in order to be submissive she refused to make any decisions, including what to serve for dinner. I looked at her in amazement and asked, "But doesn't your husband *want* you to assume some responsibility for such things? Isn't that an awful burden on him?"

She looked rather smug as she replied, "I don't know. I just want him to be the leader."

Well, that's one way to let him lead! But if a husband wants his wife to assume responsibility for the home, for agreed-upon discipline of the children, for hospitality, etc., is it submission for her to refuse? One of the tasks of a leader is to delegate so he has time and energy to lead. If those under him refuse the tasks he gives them, they're certainly not being submissive.

So exactly what is true submission? Most of us agree that submission is not a matter of superiority or inferiority. Men and women are equal in spirit, soul, mind, conscience, position, privilege, freedom, happiness, and in their walk with God. I love the quote ascribed to Augustine: "If God meant woman to rule over man, He would have taken her out of Adam's head. Had He designed her to be his slave, He would have taken her out of his feet. But God took woman out of man's side, for He made her to be a helpmate and equal to him." But there is one condition to this equality: A husband and wife are not equal in *authority* because of God's ordained arrangement of the family. A wife is to place herself under the authority of her husband, who is her leader, her protector, her "head."

True submission is not bondage. Instead, true submission leads to freedom: the freedom to be oneself, to develop one's gifts and areas of expertise, to become all God wants one to be. Now, I realize that some wives don't feel free. One woman told me she feels as though she's in prison because of the restrictions placed on her by her dictatorial husband. How sad! Obviously that husband has a wrong idea of headship. I urged that dear wife to pray that God would show her husband how wrong his ideas were, that God would show her how she might find creative alternatives to help him understand, and perhaps most of all, that God would keep her heart fixed on Jesus during this time and show her how this "prison" could conform her to His image.

When husbands *demand* submission, they are not obeying God. Wives can't demand that husbands love them like Christ loved the church, nor should husbands demand their wives submit to them. Ephesians 5:21, the verse that begins the whole discussion about husbands and wives, tells us to "submit to one another out of reverence for Christ." Both husbands and wives are to submit, and both are to love. But one of the husband's special *responsibilities* is to love, and one of the wife's special responsibilities is to submit.

BLOCKS TO SUBMISSION

The Greek word for *submit* means "to arrange under, to subordinate." It is the subjection of one individual to another, the opposite of self-assertion or of an independent, autocratic spirit. A friend of mine observed, "Submission is putting yourself wholly at the disposal of another. It is taking the best of all you are (mind, emotions, gifts, etc.) and sharing them wisely with the one over you." Submission is an attitude that says, "I'm with you and you're the boss. I will follow your decisions wholeheartedly though I may tell you of my disagreement. But once the decision has been made, I'll be with you all the way. I want to have an attitude of deferring to you, looking to you, being under your wing."

A lot of giant boulders block the road to a wife's biblical submission to her husband. I suppose the biggest one of them all is the tendency women have to manipulate.

Manipulating

In the early days of my marriage, I got quite proficient at this. When we had six people living in our home for training, two or three would come to me wondering if I'd ask Jack for certain favors: time off from the servicemen's center, the use of the car, or other special considerations. I'd wait for the right moment, explain the need, ask Jack about it, and usually get a positive response.

One day God opened my eyes to what I was doing. Though neither Jack nor I had realized it, I was manipulating him. Those young men should have discussed their desires with Jack, not me, and I shouldn't have tried to be involved in any part of it.

A wife walks a fine line here. It is wise to wait for the right moment to broach a subject. There really is a "season for everything." But if the wisdom is being used just to get our own way, it isn't wisdom; it's manipulation. We women have many manipulative methods at our disposal. We sneak a subject into the conversation when our husband feels guilty about not spending enough time with the family. We pout. We get angry. We cry. We withdraw. I've used them all in an attempt to get my own way. And sometimes I wasn't even aware of what I was doing. When I began to pray, "Lord, reveal to my heart when I'm being manipulative," God was faithful to do just that.

Rationalizing

We are good at rationalizing. I recently heard a joke that emphasizes just how far we sometimes go to get what we want. A wife was asked by her husband not to spend much money for a while, particularly on clothes, until he got out of a temporary financial bind. A few days later she came home with a new dress, and he said, "It's sure pretty, honey, but I asked you not to buy any clothes for a while, remember?" She said, "Yes, dear, but I was in the store and I saw this lovely dress, and Satan tempted me." He said, "Now dear, you know the answer to that situation. You should have said, 'Get thee behind me, Satan.'" The woman said, "I did that, dear, but when he got behind me, he said it looked beautiful from the back, too."

Many women use rationalization as a way to subvert their husband's authority. They take over certain areas in order to "help their husbands out" when, in fact, their husbands don't want to be helped out.

After taking a course in family communication, I asked a Christian family I was close to if I could interview them. We got together one evening, and after a few minutes of chitchat, I asked the husband, "How does it feel to be a member of this family?"

His response astonished me. He said, "I feel like I'm a bird on the lowest perch, and my wife has to be on a higher one." She was astonished, too!

As we talked further, he revealed that he had willingly let her take over the finances, as she was gifted in this area. However, as a result, he felt she had usurped his authority in other areas. This man is not a weak person—he's an athletic, intelligent man, a marvelous father, a dear Christian. Yet little by little over the years, he'd felt less and less like the head of his family. That evening his wife admitted her desire to control. She apologized, and with God's gracious help, things changed for that family over the next few years.

Controlling

Sometimes controlling behavior is blatant. At other times, it's so subtle we don't even realize we've assumed control.

Often we spend more time with our children than our husband does, and we assume control of parenting. It's easy to make up rules for our kids as we go along instead of talking them over with our husband. Soon he may find he doesn't even know what the regulations are around the house. Or we counter our husband's guidelines for the children behind his back, or we are slow or negligent to carry out discipline we've agreed on, or we fail to insist on rules that have been established.

One of my greatest areas of struggle is when Jack and I meet with another couple or small group. Because I can get twenty sentences in before Jack opens his mouth, the temptation to dominate is great. It grows in magnitude because many times he *wants* me to answer a question someone has asked because that gives him time to think through what he'd like to say. (He thinks. I talk.) But sometimes I find myself not merely leading the conversation when he wants me to but controlling it when no one wants me to. It's something I confess to the Lord often (much less often to Jack, I'm afraid—I hope he won't notice!).

Limits to Submission

Okay. Take a breath. Are there limits to submission? YES. (Aren't you glad?)

While a wife is to walk the road called Submission, God Himself may throw up some roadblocks along the way where she will come to a screeching halt. Always those roadblocks are raised by a clear command from God's Word. I say "clear" because some of us read into Scripture verses whatever we want to read. We interpret "Avoid all appearance of evil" as God not wanting us to accompany our husband to a baseball game on Sunday—not because we think it's against God's law but because we really don't want to go.

Submission is limited by God's specific commands. God says, "Do not commit adultery." That's a roadblock. So if your husband decides to have a wife-swapping party, you refuse. If your husband says, "Let's rob a bank together," you refuse because the roadblock of "Thou shalt not steal" is thrown up before you. If a Buddhist husband says his wife may not worship God but has to worship Buddha, his wife can say no. (She, I suppose, could accompany her husband to the Buddhist temple but could worship only the one true God.) If an insane husband says to his wife, "You *will* get me out of this hospital," the command to "bring him good, not harm, all the days of her life" (Proverbs 31:12) will take precedence over her submission to his command. But these roadblocks will be few, and if they occur, they will be definite.

What If He's Wrong?

When I was struggling with this idea of submission, a speaker in a small gathering said, "Whenever my husband does something I don't like, makes a decision I don't agree with, has a habit I'm annoyed with, I do one thing."

I waited on the edge of my chair!

She said, "I pray."

I thought, *Come on, lady. You've got to do more than that.* (At that time my philosophy was "faith without hints is dead." It was okay to pray, but "hinting"—well nagging, perhaps—and anything else I could think of to try was also necessary.)

She went on to say, "Inevitably, as I pray, one of three things happens: (1) It changes. (Prayer really does change things.) (2) My husband asks me about it. (Being "one" means sharing thoughts about everything.) Often he really hears me, and many times he changes. (3) I'm led by God to bring up the subject to him once more, and he listens. He doesn't always agree, of course, but I feel like he's really heard my point of view."

I determined to try it. And I found out she's right. It works. I discovered that after I'd really prayed about something that was bothering me, many times God just lifted it from my heart. But if He didn't, if it continued to feel like a cold, hard lump in my soul, that was my indication to bring it up again—at the right time.

After trying this for several months, I added a fourth point. Many times God showed me that I had been wrong in the first place. Imagine that! God changed *me* because I had been the one needing to change from the start.

Often I have to ask myself, *Do I push or pray? Do I belittle or build? Do I enrage or encourage? Do I forgive or frustrate?* Someone has said that even if marriages are made in heaven, people have to be responsible for the maintenance. The responsibility lasts a lifetime—and part of it, for a wife, is submission. Submission, for most of us, will never be easy. But with God as our Guide, the potholes won't swallow us, the road will be sure if not smooth, and the way will lead—believe it or not—to freedom.

Making Biblical Truth Yours

You're coming to the end, my friend. Keep up the good work! This is a tough subject, and you may be tempted to skip it. But please don't. This one is especially important to develop your own personal convictions about. So study thoughtfully:

Do the following *verse studies:*

- Ephesians 5:22-24
- Ephesians 5:33 (*Amplified Bible* if you have one)
- 1 Peter 3:1-6

Next, do a *character study* on Sarah (Genesis 12,16–23). Find out why Sarah was called a "holy woman" in 1 Peter 3:5–6.

Write one page of your personal thoughts concerning submission. What are your personal *convictions* on this subject versus your *ideas* about it? Why? Where do these convictions come from?

CHAPTER FOURTEEN

Getting Started

Essential Qualities for Discipler and Disciplee

arion opened the oven door, carefully placed two large lemon meringue pies she planned to serve her guests that evening on the top shelf, and set the timer for five minutes. As she straightened up, she glanced out the kitchen window and gasped. In slow motion the swing set on which her three-year-old son was playing wobbled, then toppled over, pinning her son underneath. Heart racing, she dashed outside, extricated Ricky from the tangled chain, poles, and boards, and assessed the damage. He was screaming and scared but had only a small scrape on his arm. She held him until his sobs quieted. Then, sitting on the grass with Ricky in her lap, she said, "Oh, honey, do you realize how God protected you? His angels watch over you, you know. Let's stop right now and thank Him for taking care of you."

Two heads bowed. Two voices rose in prayer.

And the meringues burned to a crisp.

As she came into the kitchen, Marion saw smoke pouring from around the cracks in the oven door. She turned off the oven, reached for the potholders, and took out the burned-black pies. Then she calmly scraped the burned meringue off the top, reached into the freezer for a large carton of Cool Whip, and spread it on the pies.

No wonder they say example is the best teacher. Marion was my example. Without realizing it, she taught me as I observed her life. But she also taught me deliberately by sharing her knowledge and wisdom with me. Can you be a Marion to women not quite as far along in the Christian life as you are? Yes, you can! If you've begun to grasp some of the principles in this book as well as absorb truth from church, Bible study, and godly people around you, then you can begin to have another woman walk beside you, and you can become a mentor to her.

ESSENTIAL QUALITIES OF A DISCIPLER

Yours is an extremely important task—and for a reason you may not have considered. Have you ever considered *why* Paul told Titus to have an older woman train the younger women? In the instructions to Titus, four other categories of people were to be taught directly: the older men, younger men, older women, and slaves. But the younger women were in a category all by themselves. Why?

A godly friend and teacher investigated the reasons that over two hundred male Christian workers had committed adultery with women in their church. The most common denominator was the decline of spiritual life, but the second most common cause—cited by nearly 80 percent of the respondents—was the complex relationships that were often set up as a result of counseling younger women. That's why Paul, led by the Spirit of God who is aware of all the tactics of the Enemy, said *older women* should be the ones to teach and train the younger ones.

Have you ever wondered who the "older" woman is in Titus 2? It seems to me that she is anyone a bit further along in her walk with God than the one she's helping. That means a woman in her twenties might train a woman in her forties—at least in some areas—if the younger woman has walked longer with the Lord. However, the woman Titus describes is one who has been around long enough to have marks of maturity evident in her life. It takes some time to develop godly qualities and to have the experience necessary to teach what is good.

In order to be a trainer you must have three basic things:

a heart for women,

a vision of what you want to accomplish,

and the know-how to do it.

Since you are reading this section of the book, you probably have the first two. However, let me emphasize that you can't teach what you don't know, and you can't train in things you haven't lived. The best way to teach is by example, and the only way to train is by sharing firsthand knowledge.

I once picked up an intriguing-looking book with the bold title *How to Keep Your Marriage Exciting.* I read that one way to keep romance in your marriage was to wake your husband in the morning before either of you were out of bed by smothering his face with kisses. *Before I even brush my teeth?* I thought. Reading on, my eyebrows raised even further until I turned to the back of the book to find out about this author who, I discovered, had been married less than two years. I smiled ruefully as I put the book aside. How could she tell someone married many times longer ways to keep a marriage exciting?

Knowledge can be taught by anyone of any age. My teenage granddaughter, Sunny, can teach me Spanish; she spent the first ten years of her life in Mexico. Eric, my teenage grandson, can teach me the rules of soccer, even train me how to kick a soccer ball. But neither Eric nor Sunny will ever be able to teach or train me how to be a grandmother. Only a grandmother who has walked before me is able to do that.

Mature single women can train other women in most of the areas referred to in Titus. I've seen godly single women train wives and mothers in both character and in life; they have been the "spiritual mothers" to wives. But they had to turn over the training concerning how to love and submit to husbands and how to love children to someone who had walked that road before.

GUIDELINES ON WHOM TO DISCIPLE

What kind of woman should you invest your life in? That question is every bit as important as what you want to teach and how you want to train. If you invest in women who don't really want your help, you'll soon feel like you're spinning your wheels, going nowhere. You may become discouraged about the whole process and decide it isn't for you.

Clarify What a Woman Wants or Needs

About the same time that Sonja knocked on my front door, Mary called. Her husband was having an affair, and she wanted to see me. As we talked, she said that she wanted to grow in her relationship with

God during this painful period and asked if I would help her. I thought, *I'd love to be able to do that, but I wonder what you really want. Do you need a listening ear? A counselor? An adopted grandmother for your kids? I'd love to help you grow spiritually, but is that what you have in mind? You see, the "Titus" kind of relationship is more than temporary help; it is building into a life. I'm not sure that's what you want.*

A picture came to mind: A home's foundation has been laid, and the walls are ready to be put up. But during the night the wind blows a pile of leaves onto the foundation, and the builder spends his time sweeping off the leaves. The following morning the builder discovers someone has thrown garbage on the slab, so he spends the day cleaning up the garbage. And so it goes throughout the weeks and months, and the walls of the structure are never raised.

So it is with many lives. The foundation—Jesus Christ (1 Corinthians 3:11)—has been laid, but if we spend all our time dealing with problems, the walls that could prevent the leaves, garbage, snow, and rain from coming in will never be built. Walls must be put up— walls such as a growing knowledge and depth in the Word of God, knowing how to pray, commitment to obeying what God says—even as problems are dealt with.

My mental picture faded, and I focused on the woman before me. I wondered if Mary wanted help with the garbage or help to build walls, and so I suggested she do some specific things to assist in her growth and to call me when she finished.

I never heard from her again.

Leave the Initiative Up to Her

I realize that counseling, listening, and lifting a load in various ways are not only important in and of themselves but are important parts of the building process. However, I need to determine as early as possible what a person really wants and the degree of her commitment and involvement. One way to find these out is to suggest a simple study—one that will help her not only with her problem but will also begin the building process. While I'm tempted to say, "Let's meet next week to talk again and go over what you've done," I try instead to leave the initiative with the seeker and say, "Call me when you're finished, and we'll get together."

There are two reasons for this: One, I want to find out if she's the kind of woman who is a learner—one who means it when she says she wants to grow and who will pay the price in time and discipline to do that. Don't forget the DGIWTH principle: "Don't get involved with the halfhearted." Two, I know that my words—even backed by some experience and knowledge—are not what will cause growth in a woman's life. Only God can do that, and He does it primarily through His Word. So if the person isn't willing to open herself to Him and dig into Scripture, I am greatly limited in my ability to help.

Look for FAT Women

I encourage you to look—and pray—for FAT women: women who are F-faithful, A-available, and T-teachable. When God brings a woman like that into your life, grab her! She may not know exactly what she wants or who she wants it from, but she is obviously seeking to go deeper with God and wants to learn. Ask her out for lunch or coffee just to get to know her. As you become acquainted, share your own experience—either how you wished you'd had a mentor (if you didn't) or how having one helped you. Ask if anyone has helped her in areas of spiritual growth, and see how God leads from there.

Encouragement for Your Walk Together

I hope this book has given you plenty of insight into what you can offer some of the less spiritually mature women in your life. If you've absorbed a part of the content and done the studies, you have in your hands a place to begin and some fairly simple "pass-on-able" tools of Bible study. I trust God won't allow you to get discouraged in this task.

At a low point of my life I read the story of the widow whose sons were about to be sold into slavery because she couldn't pay her debts (2 Kings 4:1-7). She cried out to Elisha for help, and Elisha asked, "How can I help you? Tell me, what do you have in your house?"

"Your servant has nothing there at all," she said, "except a little oil."

As I read those words, I felt like weeping. You see, I was feeling as bereft as that widow. I felt like I didn't have anything to give—no talent or gift with which to serve the Lord. For the millionth time, I was feeling like a failure. But God was speaking. He was saying to me, as Elisha said to that widow woman, "What do you have in your house?" And I was answering as she did, "Your servant has nothing there at all." But even as the widow added, "except a little oil," I added, "Well, I have this little message I long to share with women."

You remember what happened. Elisha asked the widow to borrow all her neighbors' empty jars—a lot of them. Then, after shutting the doors, she was to begin pouring the little bit of oil into the jars. She poured and poured and poured—until all the jars were full. She sold the oil, redeemed her sons, and lived on the rest of the money. She believed, obeyed, and began.

Following her example, I said, "All right, Lord. I give my little bit of oil—this message I have on my heart for women—to You. Will You multiply it?" That was before I wrote my first book, before I began speaking at women's conferences. *Before*. God has taken my little bit of oil and multiplied it beyond what I ever imagined He would. And let me tell you, it has all been *His* doing.

Discipling someone means helping her become everything a godly woman should be. Generally, many people are involved in this process, and we should be grateful for the privilege of putting even one board of the building into place. In most cases we will step into someone's life, minister in some small way, and step out. We need not think that if we've helped only in a limited part of someone's life, we've failed. We must remember that it is the Holy Spirit who is the ultimate Builder, Helper, Counselor, and Mentor. He will fit all the pieces together. You need only to begin your small part.

Making Biblical Truth Yours

As a woman whom God has called to help someone else, your task will be to keep on growing . . . and growing . . . and growing. Here's a list of studies on various subjects to help you do that.

On the Character of a Godly Woman
Do the following *verse studies* on the character of a godly woman:

- Proverbs 14:1
- Proverbs 12:4
- Proverbs 31:26,30

Do a *character study* on:

- Ruth (book of Ruth), listing the ways Naomi helped Ruth become a godly woman
- Abigail (1 Samuel 25)

Study the characteristics of the tongue. Begin with James 3. Then use a concordance to look up words such as *tongue, words, mouth*. List what our speech should be and what it shouldn't be. Do a personal application on one area about which you feel God is speaking to your heart.

Read a book on the tongue. Joseph Stowell's *Tongue in Check* (Victor Books) or my book *Words That Hurt, Words That Heal* (NavPress) may be a place to begin.

Read through the book of John, writing down characteristics of Christ. Pick one on which to do a *topical study*.

Go through *The Life and Times of Jesus Christ* Bible study series (NavPress).

On Prayer

Read John 17, and list the subjects of Christ's prayer for His disciples. What are the universals that we should pray for those we love?

Do a *topical study* of prayer considering what we should pray for, when we should pray, how we should pray, to whom we should pray, etc.

Study Philippians 1:9-11 and Ephesians 1:17-19, and write out what Paul prayed for those people. Make a *prayer list* for your husband, children, friends, and those you are helping, following Paul's example of what to pray for.

Finally, don't hesitate to ask "older" women to continue to mentor *you*. If you need help learning to pray, get together with a prayer warrior in your church, and ask for help.

CHAPTER FIFTEEN

And Now the Nitty-Gritty

What to Do When You Get Together

One of my favorite stories is about the man who borrowed a book from his friend and was intrigued both by the parts underlined and the initials written in the margins—YBH. He puzzled over this until he returned the book to his friend and asked him about the strange initials beside the underlining. His friend smiled and said, "Well, basically I agree with the underlined sections. The YBH stands for 'Yes, but *how?*'"

I've always been a "how?" person. If you're like me, you might need some more concrete "how-to-start-and-continue" instructions for discipling a younger woman. Here are a few.

WHEN AND WHERE?

It's best to meet each week, if possible, but every other week is fine, too. The actual times aren't as important as the consistency, regularity, and commitment to those times.

Your home is probably the best place to meet (with your phone off the hook). But if she has to meet when her small children are napping, her home may be the right choice. If interruptions are constant at both of your homes, meet at a restaurant or neutral location. One or both of you may have to put your children in a church nursery for a "mothers' day out" or get a sitter, but it's important to have a place where distractions are minimal.

HOW?

After you've established that she really is serious in her desire for spiritual help, have her bring a list of her written goals and personal needs as well as what she wants or expects from this mentoring relationship. Then share with her an overall view of where you'd like to head over the next four (or six or eight) weeks. (You should have on paper what you'd like to see in her life over the next two years, but short-term objectives don't seem so overwhelming and may be useful while you continue to determine if she really is a faithful, teachable, available person.) Your list of short-term goals will be revised frequently as you determine her personal needs. After the first month or two, if you are both excited about learning together, then you can suggest an extended period of teaching and training with other definite goals in mind.

You can disciple women one-on-one or in small groups. Three or four women can stimulate one another and often become friends who walk beside each other as they grow. At one point when I was meeting individually with several women a week, I realized that I was going over the same material with each of them because they were all in about the same place spiritually. So every other week we decided to meet as a small group to go over those basics of growth, and during the "free" week I met individually with each one to be sure she was personally grasping and digesting the material.

WHAT?

Because you are working with an individual, what you want to cover will vary. You might start with a felt need such as the difficulty she's having as a mother or the anger she's experiencing because of a broken relationship. At some point, however, it is crucial to move from her pressing felt need to what is essential for growth in every believer. Don't be fooled into thinking that merely dealing with life problems is discipleship. And when you are working with problems or felt needs, be sure you're building strong spiritual walls and not just sweeping garbage off the foundation. Walls are built by letting the Word answer the problems, by praying together and separately, and by helping your friend see that it is God alone who really can deal with her difficulties.

My initial goal for each woman I disciple is to develop her maturity and confidence in the following areas:

- assurance of salvation (1 John 5:11,13)
- how to spend daily time with God (quiet time)
- making Christ the center of her life
- the importance of the Word of God
- methods of taking in God's Word (hearing, reading, studying, memorizing, meditating, applying)
- prayer
- obedience

- the importance of fellowship (church, study groups, other believers)
- how to give a personal testimony
- how to share the gospel with unbelievers
- how to know God's will
- how to develop faith
- serving the body of Christ
- giving
- vital doctrines: e.g., the Trinity, sin, Satan, etc.
- character issues, including purity, holiness, self-control, kindness, jealousy, envy, fruit of the Spirit (Galatians 5:22-23), being a godly wife, loving her children, managing her home

There's also an interesting minilist in Titus 2:3, even before the verses on specific qualities the older women are to teach the younger women. This list includes reverence, not being a slanderer, not being addicted to much wine, and being able to teach what is good—all wonderful qualities to keep in mind when determining needs. With some women, it might be necessary to include topics such as determining gifts, worship, ministry proficiency, and self-development (appearance, manners, etc.).

AND WHEN YOU MEET TOGETHER . . .

Each session should include study of God's Word and prayer. Even if you don't finish discussing the assigned study, it's crucial to do a part of it for growth as well as accountability. Regarding prayer, never force a person to pray until she is ready—especially in a small group. This can intimidate and frighten some women to the point that they'll never come again. When I teach prayer, I say to a person or group (after several times of being together), "Think of one thing you are thankful for. Just one." (Then I wait for them to do this.) "Now, let's tell the Lord out loud that one thing, saying, 'Thank You, Lord, for . . .'" I pray first, keeping it to one sentence, such as, "Thank You, Lord, for Your Son."

Goals and accountability are essential. If a woman rarely does the study you've suggested, your relationship should be reevaluated and changed. It could be changed to friendship without teaching ("Let's just get together for lunch once a month"), or it should be terminated. Because it is God's Word, not ours, that causes growth and change, there is little point of continuing to try to disciple a person who won't commit to the studies and the accountability vital to her growth.

To summarize, in each session you'll strive to:

- motivate and encourage
- talk over the study that has been done and discuss your ideas about it
- give another study to do for the next time period
- pray together

You'll want to keep a record of the dates you've met, what study has been done, what assignment has been given for the next time, and what you've talked about. Make notes to yourself about what questions you want to ask the next time you get together, such as, "What happened when you called that person? How did it go with . . . ? How did God answer our prayer about . . . ?"

CONCERNS YOU MAY HAVE

I wish so much that we could sit down together, because I'm sure you have some concerns. I think one of my main concerns was, How can I ever teach and train and mentor when there's so much I need to learn myself? Please don't be discouraged. Each and every one of us is an imperfect and sinful woman, but that mustn't stop us from doing what God tells us to do.

I recall an incident at the first training home we lived in, where Jack and I were responsible to help younger men and women with their lives and character. Jack wanted to talk to one of the men who lived with us about a negative characteristic he had observed in Al's life. At the same time, Jack watched Al's faithfulness in his time with the Lord. Al got up at five o'clock every morning to spend at least an hour in the Word, and then he'd walk around and around the block praying.

Jack asked a mentor-friend about the situation, "How can I talk to Al about his problem when he is so much more consistent in his time with God than I am?"

Bob answered, "If I waited to talk to someone until I had everything perfect, I'd never talk to anyone about anything."

Jack got the point. Except for the Lord Jesus Himself, all of us have areas of weakness on which God is working. Nevertheless, God can use us to help others in areas where we may have more insight or be a bit stronger. If we waited until we had it all together, we would fail to obey Matthew 28:19-20 where the Lord Jesus commanded, "Go and make disciples of all nations."

Another concern you may have is, It will cost too much. You know, you're right about the cost. Discipling women has no financial return; instead of getting paid, you pay. You pay in time, in energy, in empathy, and yes, sometimes in heartache as you experience rejection from someone you've poured your life into. The world has seduced us into thinking success is spelled "money" and "position." God spells success "obedience."

Do you have the time? Probably not. You won't *have* the time; you must *make* the time. And in order to do that, your priorities will have to be evaluated and sometimes changed. Sometimes we get so busy doing good things—organizing outreach luncheons, women's conferences, canvassing for the cancer society—that we often neglect one of the best things God commands us to do: to go and make disciples.

In her book *Women Encouraging Women*, Lucibel VanAtta offers a helpful acrostic for our times with others:

A—appreciating and applauding others
S—studying their needs
M—modeling the qualities they seek
I—imparting enthusiasm as a way of life
L—listening in a careful and caring way
E—expecting them to succeed
We can do it with a *smile*.[1]

Friend, God can and will use your life in a significant way as you grow to be more like Jesus and as the desire of your heart becomes to pass on what you know of Him to women everywhere.

Prior to World War II, a young pharmacist moved with his wife to a small town in South Dakota called Wall. Wall is miles from anywhere and a half-mile off the main highway, so business was sparse, and the pharmacy was going broke.

One day the pharmacist's wife went out in their backyard to get a bucket of cold water from their deep well. As she pulled out the bucket, she contemplated the cars whizzing by on the distant highway and wondered what she and her husband could do to get some of them to stop. An idea occurred to her.

She went into the drugstore and said to her husband, "You know, perhaps if we made signs to put on the highway advertising free ice water, some cars might stop." Her husband laughed, but since they had absolutely nothing to lose by trying, the next day they hand-lettered signs that said, "Free Ice Water! Wall Drug Store, Wall, South Dakota" and put them up along the main road. And sure enough, a few cars stopped, and the occupants sheepishly asked for their free ice water. When they got it, a number would buy something else they needed.

Encouraged, the young couple put up more signs, and more people stopped. Then professionally made signs were posted one hundred miles in each direction, drawing hoards of people to the drugstore. Today that husband and wife are retired millionaires, and their children have taken over the drugstore, now expanded to include a restaurant, gift shops, and a whole collection of other touristy attractions.[2]

How did they do it? They started where they were (Wall, South Dakota), used what they had (ice water), and did what they could.

So, my friend, can you!

CHAPTER TWO

1. Dr. Paul Brand and Philip Yancey, *Fearfully and Wonderfully Made* (Grand Rapids, Mich.: Zondervan, 1980), 45-46.

CHAPTER FOUR

1. The Topical Memory System can be ordered from NavPress, P.O. Box 35001, Colorado Springs, CO 80935, (800) 525-7151. The Bible Memory Association has great systems for Scripture memory, too. Either of these systems can be ordered through a Christian bookstore.
2. Joseph Bayly, *Psalms of My Life* (Wheaton, Ill.: Tyndale, 1971), 53.

CHAPTER FIVE

1. A. W. Tozer, *The Root of the Righteous* (Harrisburg, Pa.: Christian Publications, 1955), 49-50.

CHAPTER SIX

1. Hannah Whitall Smith, *The Christian's Secret of a Happy Life* (Uhrichsville, Ohio: Barbour & Company, Inc., 1985), 47-48.
2. Ann Landers, *The Gazette Telegraph*, 30 September 1996.

CHAPTER SEVEN

1. John D. Davis, *A Dictionary of the Bible* (Grand Rapids, Mich.: Baker, 1954), 822.
2. Dr. Ed Wheat, *Love-Life for Every Married Couple* (Grand Rapids, Mich.: Zondervan, 1980), 182.
3. Dr. Willard F. Harley Jr., *His Needs, Her Needs* (Grand Rapids, Mich.: Revell, 1986).
4. Linda Dillow, *Creative Counterpart* (Nashville, Tenn.: Nelson, 1977), 97.

CHAPTER TEN

1. W. E. Vine, *Expository Dictionary of New Testament Words*, vol. 4 (Old Tappan, N. J.: Revell, 1966), 44.
2. Vine, *Expository Dictionary*, 44.

CHAPTER FIFTEEN

1. Lucibel VanAtta, *Women Encouraging Women* (Portland, Ore.: Multnomah, 1987), 73.
2. Jack Mayhall, *The Price and the Prize* (Wheaton, Ill.: Victor, 1985), 139-40.